Hebrews

Preaching the Word

Smyth & Helwys Publishing, Inc.
6316 Peake Road
Macon, Georgia 31210-3960
1-800-747-3016
©2020 by Anne Scalfaro and Andrew Daugherty
All rights reserved.

Library of Congress Cataloging-in-Publication Data

Names: Scalfaro, Anne, author. | Daugherty, Andrew, author.
Title: Hebrews / by Anne Scalfaro and Andrew Daugherty.
Description: Macon, GA : Smyth & Helwys Publishing, 2021. | Series: Preaching the Word | Includes bibliographical references.
Identifiers: LCCN 2020052290 (print) | LCCN 2020052291 (ebook) | ISBN 9781641730921 (paperback) | ISBN 9781641732468 (ebook)
Subjects: LCSH: Bible. Hebrews--Commentaries.
Classification: LCC BS2775.53 .S28 2021 (print) | LCC BS2775.53 (ebook) | DDC 227/.8707--dc23
LC record available at https://lccn.loc.gov/2020052290
LC ebook record available at https://lccn.loc.gov/2020052291

Disclaimer of Liability: With respect to statements of opinion or fact available in this work of nonfiction, Smyth & Helwys Publishing Inc. nor any of its employees, makes any warranty, express or implied, or assumes any legal liability or responsibility for the accuracy or completeness of any information disclosed, or represents that its use would not infringe privately-owned rights.

Praise for *Preaching the Word: Hebrews*

The word "creative" is something of an understatement in describing this collection of dialogue sermons preached jointly through the book of Hebrews by Anne Scalfaro and Andrew Daugherty. But so would words like "insightful," "inspirational," "prophetic" and oh yes, "gospel." Read the sermons closely; and read them all.

—Bill J. Leonard
Professor of Divinity Emeritus, Wake Forest University

Like the Book of Hebrews itself that proclaims Jesus as the fullest revelation of God's sympathy for and saving of a sinful and suffering humanity, Anne Scalfaro and Andrew Daugherty re-present the good news with a freshness and fleshiness that heals and helps. For the biblical scholar and the spiritual starter alike, whether in the pulpit or the pew, these words ring true.

—Rev. Dr. George A. Mason
Senior Pastor, Wilshire Baptist Church, Dallas, TX

Might there be a better theme for our world, let alone for a contemporary commentary volume? A study of the Letter to the Hebrews entitled "Raising Hope" provides an onramp to exactly the virtue the body of Christ needs. In a time when hope seems to be in short supply, Anne Scalfaro and Andrew Daughtery add fresh insight into the whereabouts of hope and how their readers might avail themselves of this essential quality. Students of this commentary are encouraged to find hope in "God's never-ending and never-changing love" and correction for a faith that flags "when hope is lost." If you are looking for a new way to cast hope in your preaching and in your life, you have found a timely resource, one filled with treasure and hope.

—Rev. Dr. Zina Jacque
Pastor Community Church of Barrington, IL

Anne Scalfaro and Andrew Daugherty have gifted us as readers with a commentary that makes an ancient, enigmatic epistle preach-able and applicable to life and faith today. With prophetic and pastoral skill they invite readers to explore the theology and hope of this first century congregation and how with such theology and hope we can live into God's kin-dom in better and stronger ways today.

—Rev. Dr. Brian J. Henderson
Senior Minister, First Baptist Church of Denver, Denver, CO

A brilliant resource that nourishes faith, challenges assumptions, and raises hope. Anne Scalfaro and Andrew Daugherty deftly guide us into the heart of Hebrews. Their splendidly crafted sermons are filled with fresh insights and illustrations of the authors' conviction that by clinging to Christ, we can be living imprints of God's love, grace, and hope. In relevant ways we are inspired to go deeper into knowing who we are and who we are meant to be.

— Rev. Mary Armacost Hulst
Pastor Emerita, Calvary Baptist Church of Denver

Hebrews

Anne Scalfaro
Andrew Daugherty

Contents

Preface	ix
Introduction	xv
1. Making a Good Impression	1
2. Getting Down to Earth	11
3. Lighten Up: It Doesn't Have to be This Way	21
4. Reclaiming Rest	29
5. Not Afraid to Ask for Help	41
6. Preschool or PhD: Where Are You in the School of Faith?	53
7. Anchored by Hope	59
8. King Melchizedek (It's Okay, No One Else Knows who He is Either)	69
9. Jesus: The People's Priest	79
10. At-one-ment, Part One: A Sacrifice Worth Saving?	91
11. At-one-ment, Part Two: Accepting Forgiveness Once and for All	101
12. Whole-hearted Faith	115
13. The Fantasy that Faith Requires	123
14. The Face at the Finish Line	133
15. Shaking Things Up	139
16. Here's the Heart of It	149

Preface

It's been five years since Andrew and I wrote and preached this sixteen-week sermon series we entitled, *Raising Hope: The Heart of Hebrews.* In those years, some things have changed. Andrew and I no longer serve the same church together. Calvary Baptist Church of Denver, where I still serve, is in a healthier, more stable place than we were five years ago (chapter 16 reminds me of just how far we've come). I am also a wiser pastor as I've journeyed with this community for five more years, bringing our tenure together to twelve years together this fall. We are in the midst of a pandemic, learning what it means to *be* the church without gathering together weekly, as we worship virtually. This new preaching experience, involving recording and production skills none of us knew we had until now, also requires a more intimate preaching voice and presence that carries into the living rooms of both our congregants and an increasingly wider 'virtual' audience who is tuning into our services each week.

Other things haven't changed. Andrew and I are still friends and colleagues. We have the utmost respect for one another and we serve sister churches just miles apart in Colorado. Racial injustice and systemic racism still persist. The massacre at Mother Emanuel AME Church in Charleston, SC in June 2015, which we speak to in chapters five and seven, was the result of racist, white supremacist beliefs as evidenced in one individual. Those beliefs have been emboldened over the past five years and are now seen more broadly and clearly by people across our country. As I write this in early August 2020, protests which began in late May continue to fill the streets of cities across our country; they are driven by outrage over systemic racism and police brutality as evidenced in the deaths of Elijah McClain (August 2019), Breonna Taylor (March 2020), and George Floyd (May 2020), to name three of the Black lives lost at the hands of law enforcement. The need for Christian communities to *be* the church outside of the walls of our sanctuaries is stronger than ever, not just because of the pandemic but because the radical, justice-seeking, inclusive love of Christ is a message of hope and transformation that our divided and broken country needs. And we, the individual people who strive to hold on to faith in such tumultuous times, need it as well.

In re-reading these sermons, I am struck by three insights that will remain with me from this project. I'll discuss each one, then provide my central take away of each insight First, Hebrews is a dense and intense thirteen-chapter sermon that does not shy away from deep theological questions or from revisiting the people's heritage as told through the biblical narrative even as the author/preacher seeks to ignite faith in its jaded and disinterested listeners. **Take away:** Critical thinking, biblical knowledge, and the stories of our ancestors are key components to a lasting faith.

Second, the writer/preacher of Hebrews calls on people to use their *minds* (theological inquiry) and their *hearts* (stories from their ancestors and the 'cloud of witnesses') to understand their faith and the meaning of Jesus Christ's message and mission. But he doesn't stop there; he makes no apologies in challenging the people to use their minds and hearts to put their faith into *action* (show love and hospitality). **Take away:** A living and persisting faith involves the head, heart, and hands (thinking, feeling, and doing).

Third, the writer/preacher of Hebrews always comes back to hope. The preacher inspires hope in the Christ who calls us to seek a more loving, inclusive, justice-seeking world through means of hard work (persistence in the race), reclaiming rest, and ultimately, always remembering that we are created in the beloved image of our Creator. The preacher of Hebrews *informs* and *inspires*, leading us all to hold onto hope, as evidenced in the person of Jesus Christ and as embodied by each and every listener and person of faith, from generation to generation. **Take away:** Hope doesn't just happen; it has to be remembered, taught, and lived out. Hope has to be raised; *that's* the heart of Hebrews.

When I write, particularly as it relates to issues of racial injustice, I am writing as a white, straight woman, so when I say there are things in our country that are broken and we have work to do, the "we" is referring to white, privileged people such as myself. This is not always explicitly clear, and I want to ensure the readers that I am never implying that people of color haven't been doing this work for generations and generations.

As you will see, I owe a great deal of gratitude to many scholars who helped me understand and make sense of Hebrews, which honestly is a difficult and obtuse read at times. My sermons especially leaned heavily into the scholarship of Tom Long's commentary on Hebrews; I recognize this and am deeply grateful for the homiletical lens with which he writes.

In chapter sixteen, as I write about my beloved faith community of Calvary Baptist Church of Denver, much has changed in terms of where our congregation is in our volunteering and commitment and financial giving. And of course, now in the pandemic, we are learning what it means to *be* church in a whole new way. It strikes me how differently I would write that final sermon today. But the exercise remains the same; all of us as preachers, including the preacher of Hebrews, write to our listeners at a *certain point in time*. These sermons are not meant for all times or all communities. They are specific and personal, even as the over-arching truths remain. And such is true for me in chapter sixteen; I hope readers will be able to read how the preacher of Hebrews concludes his sermon with an exhortation to action and a benediction of blessing, and do the same as they preach to their congregations.

And in conclusion, I extend my deep gratitude to:

Smyth & Helwys, for the invitation to embark on this project.

Andrew Daugherty, for your collegiality, friendship, and authenticity. You were the perfect partner for this project.

Calvary Baptist Church of Denver, for your grace, endurance, and enthusiasm on being a part of this preaching experiment, and for my colleagues at Calvary who helped Andrew and I have the space and time (inside and outside of the pulpit) to pull this off—especially Morgan C. Fletcher and Michelle Honeycutt.

Coffee at the Point, an extraordinary space in Five Points in Denver. Andrew and I met every Thursday at Coffee at the Point for four months straight for hours at a time, and we are grateful for their delicious food and drink and even more for their hospitality and welcome in allowing us to reserve space to work on this project with commentaries spread out and laptops plugged in.

George Mason, for "raising hope" in me as a young person growing up at Wilshire Baptist Church in Dallas, TX, helping me discern my call to ministry, mentoring me through the pastoral residency program, and encouraging me every step of the way—including now, as your colleague in ministry. Your prophetic and pastoral voice, more than any other, has most shaped my preaching voice.

My parents, who are my biggest fans in life and in ministry, and who first introduced me to the love and hope of Jesus and the beauty and importance of church community.

Damon, my husband, who embodies what it means to be a faithful, loving partner, who gets excited to learn about the stories of Scripture, and who always makes sure I have time to "shut it down" and pull away from work—which is important for my sanity and my soul. I am able to be a pastor because of Damon's presence, support, and love.

God, the Mystery of all Mysteries, whose love and grace allows my humanity to be enough, and in whom I place my hope and my faith, my doubts and my questions, and of course, my calling.

Anne Scalfaro

I extend my gratitude to:

Anne Scalfaro, for modeling to me the best of pastoral leadership and for your invitation to partner with you in this preaching project. Your collegiality and friendship have saved my life in more ways than I can say.

Calvary Baptist Church of Denver, for being a community of grace to me and my family and for entrusting me to be your first-ever *Executive Pastor*.

Pine Street Church of Boulder, for calling me to be your senior pastor since this book endeavor concluded and for being the people of God who embrace everyone, inspire life, and create more.

George Mason, for believing in me as a pastor and preacher before I believed in myself. You have shown me how being fully human and "doing what I do" make the best vocational match. (And for always finding humor in my imitations of you).

Addison and Aidan, my children, who are my spiritual shamans and my two heartbeats always. I am raising you, but you are "raising hope" in me everyday. I am never closer to God than when I am close to you.

Andrew Daugherty

Introduction

This summer we are writing a commentary on the New Testament book of Hebrews. To be published by Smyth & Helwys, this will be one volume in a commentary series by preachers across the United States called *Preaching the Word*. Unlike traditional biblical commentaries that focus strictly on a biblical book's history and intent, this series is designed for us all to be hearers and participants in Scripture. The goal is an experience that is more personal to our lives. The commentary series is unique because it's composed of preached sermons in the context of a real-life faith community, which means that you, Calvary, play a vital role in the project itself.

The parameters we've been given include that it must be an extended, uninterrupted sermon series covering every verse of every chapter in the book of Hebrews. In other words, we can't skip the hard parts! This summer's preaching series that we have titled "Raising Hope: The Heart of Hebrews" will begin on Pentecost Sunday and run through the summer until the week before Gathering Sunday.

Scholars agree that Hebrews has one of the most sophisticated theologies in the New Testament, and therefore is one of the hardest books for the modern reader to understand. But fear not! We have accepted the creative challenge of making Hebrews relatable to our world today, relevant for our life together at Calvary, and spiritually enriching for us all.

Can't wait to share this experience with you,

Anne & Andrew

Making a Good Impression

Hebrews 1:1–2:4

Pentecost Sunday, Memorial Day Weekend
The first chapter of Hebrews reminds us that God has been raising hope among God's people long before we were here through the voices of the Hebrew prophets, the life and love of Jesus, and the mysterious messages of the angels. For Christians, the most impressive of these voices is Jesus—the One who bears the "imprint of God's very being" (1:3). These voices help us understand ourselves as "impressions of Jesus" and what that means for the messages we tell ourselves and others.

Anne: After reading this first chapter of Hebrews, you're probably thinking, "Maybe I'll just take the summer off from church." To be honest with you, when Andrew and I sat down a few weeks ago to start working on this sermon series, we looked at each other and thought, "Maybe we'll just take the summer off from preaching!"

But here we are in Hebrews. And why are we here, you ask? About a year and a half ago, Smyth & Helwys contacted me to see if I would be interested in preaching through a book of the Bible that would then become a volume in the homiletical commentary series, *Preaching the Word*. Excited about the chance to focus on things I love—preaching and writing—and flattered by the offer, I said, "Sure!" They said, "Great! Do you want Hebrews or Revelation?" So you see, it could have been way worse! You should be thanking me that we're not spending all summer in Revelation.

It only took one read through of Hebrews for me to write Smyth & Helwys and say, "So . . . can I co-write this with my colleague, Andrew? We did this Advent preaching series back and forth that went over really well with our congregation." (Essentially, I didn't want to tackle this book alone. What's that saying, "misery loves company"?) Smyth & Helwys said, "Sure, why not," and then I asked Andrew and he said, "Sure, why not," (thanks be to God), and so here we are.

And here you are. Because, you see, the nature of this project is contextual. Meaning, we have to preach through every verse of Hebrews—we can't skip the hard parts—and we have to preach to a real, live congregation. So, while we know you didn't have any say in the matter, you're now part of this marathon adventure with us. And it will be just that—a marathon. But fear not! We've accepted the creative challenge of making Hebrews relatable to our world today, relevant for our life together, and spiritually enriching for us all.

When you dive into Hebrews, while much of it is hard to understand at first, it's clear that the promise and gift of *hope* rises up from its pages. The hope from God at the heart of Hebrews raises a hope within our own hearts that will embolden our faith and revitalize our lives.

It may feel at times like we're trudging through muddy waters, but trust us, there's hope on the other side. In fact, there's hope all along the way. We really believe that by the end of this series, this hope will have a hold on you, and on all of us. The tenacious and enduring nature of this hope is reflected well in a quote from the French writer, Albert Camus, who, by the way, is most well known for the type of philosophy known as "absurdism" (go figure):

> In the midst of winter, I found there was, within me, an invincible summer. And that makes me happy. For it says that no matter how hard the world pushes against me, within me, there's something stronger—something better, pushing right back.[1]

Thus begins our invincible summer together: raising hope in our lives, letting the heart of Hebrews shape our faith, and having fun along the way.

Andrew: And so, when was the last time you remember hearing a sermon based on any Scripture in the book of Hebrews? (Me, either.) Hebrews gets caught in a kind of biblical black hole—we don't preach on it much because we don't hear it preached on very much. It has largely dropped out of use in many churches. Even though it is a book in the New Testament, it just sits there unnoticed. Here's the thing, though: Hebrews contains one of the New Testament's most sophisticated discussions of the meaning of Jesus for the life of faith.

This is a fascinating feature, because the book addresses real-life human problems all people, including us, are bound to face. See if you identify with any of this: the original hearers of Hebrews are spiritually exhausted, they probably feel stuck in their prayer lives, they're thinking about walking away from the faith altogether, and they are even disenchanted with Jesus.[2]

Apparently, if you think of Hebrews as a kind of speech or sermon, which some scholars do, the preacher of Hebrews thinks, given all of this, that it's a good idea to speak to the congregation in complex theological language about the meaning of Jesus' death and resurrection. Perhaps this is a big reason why Hebrews has been so neglected—it's complex, it requires patience to read and understand, and all of its rich imagery and lofty poetic images can leave our heads spinning.

As far as who the author or preacher of Hebrews is, this believer whom we have to thank for all this head-spinning spiritual treasure, well, it remains a mystery even to theological masters. After guessing about who wrote Hebrews, even Origen, the smartest biblical scholar in the ancient world, concluded: God only knows!

Some in the ancient world believed it was St. Paul, which may be why Hebrews made it into the New Testament in the first place. There have been lots of theories and guesses about who the writer is, but nothing is conclusive. We also don't know very much about who the first readers were (Gentiles? Jews? A mixture?) or where they were (Rome? Jerusalem? Colossae?).[3]

Many modern scholars believe the audience was Jewish Christians who lived in a city (since the writer refers to the city in chapter 13).

Honesty requires us to admit that we don't have sure and certain answers about these circumstances. What endures, though, is the usefulness and truthfulness of its spiritual wisdom about what it means to follow God in the way of Jesus.

Anne: My husband Damon is my litmus test when it comes to biblical knowledge. I grew up Baptist with lots of Bible; he grew up Catholic with not much Bible at all. So I check to see what he knows or doesn't know, and that tells me how much 'splaining I need to do in a sermon. When I asked him, "Do you know what Hebrews is?" He answered, "Isn't that, like, the Old Testament?" (Sigh.)

Actually though, Damon isn't so far off because Hebrews quotes 737 words of the Old Testament—which is 15% of its complete content, more than any other New Testament book. The author's mind was "marinated in the Old Testament."[4] In other words, the Christian theology in Hebrews is not laid out on a blank canvas. Rather, it's layered on top of an already multilayered theology of first century Judaism. And you can see this influence from the beginning as the author talks about the ways that God has been speaking in the world: "Long ago God spoke to our ancestors in many and various ways by the prophets" (1:1). And then, a bit later, we read, "Are not all angels spirits in the divine service? . . . [For if] the message of the angels was valid . . ." (1:14a, 2:2a).

The author is clear that in order for us to understand how Christ uniquely speaks something of God to us, we have to first understand that God has been speaking since the dawn of time. God spoke creation into being: "Let there be light," (Gen 1:3) and God spoke through many signs and wonders, from the roar of a burning bush in the desert (Ex 3) to the sound of sheer silence on a mountainside (1 Kings 19).

And God spoke through messengers, namely prophets and angels. Prophets and angels both gave powerful, transforming messages, but they did so in two different ways and they had two different audiences. The prophets—people like Isaiah, Micah, Jeremiah, and Amos—spoke to God's people at large. Their message was rarely a comforting one because it was usually delivered in response to the people failing to hold up their end of God's covenant with them. The prophets called people to justice or some kind of collective action: "But let justice roll down like waters, and righteousness like an ever-flowing stream" (Amos 5:24).

Angels did the opposite. Angels spoke messages to individuals, usually in dreams and almost always one-on-one with no one else around. Angels gave messages of hope in personal situations where reassurance or direction was needed. An angel appeared to Hagar and her son Ishmael as they fled from Abraham and Sarah, assuring Hagar that she would live and be blessed (Gen 16:10). An angel wrestled Jacob on the banks of the Jabbok River, giving him both a limp and a new name as he prepared to face his estranged brother Esau (Gen 32:28).

You see, the author of Hebrews reminds us that God has been speaking to humanity through prophets and angels, then prepares us for the new voice through which God is speaking: Jesus Christ. Jesus speaks in the ways of the prophets and the angels, combining the best of both worlds. He speaks a prophetic message of love to the society and culture of his day on a communal level, and he spends his ministry speaking into the individual lives of people, healing them from their unique ailments, listening to their life stories, sitting around their kitchen tables, fishing in their personal boats.

Jesus embodies both the communal voice of the prophets and the personal voice of the angels. Thus, he comes as the voice of God to us in a completely new way.

Andrew: "He is the reflection of God's glory and the exact imprint of God's very being" (Heb 1:3a). This is a stunning spiritual statement. Right away we hear an often-repeated assertion in Hebrews that what God is, the Son is. This is to say, what we see and hear and experience of Jesus is a totally trustworthy revelation of the heart of God. What is *in* Jesus is *in* God and there is nothing in Jesus' nature that is contrary to God or who God is. What is present and active in the Son is nothing less than God. Because if Jesus is less than God, how can we ever say that what we see and observe in Jesus is trustworthy with regard to God's nature?

Remember how, when angels appear in Scripture, they usually introduce themselves by saying, "Fear not!"? When God set out to make an impression on the world, God did this through the human impression of Jesus. And with this human impression, Jesus shows us that, there is nothing to fear with God. And this truth can be trusted. And what's more, we hear in these lofty, poetic, cosmic images used throughout Hebrews that there's a beautiful unity of the divine and the human in the one who is called the Son.

He is the reflection of God's glory and the exact imprint of God's very being, and he sustains all things by his powerful word (1:3).

Right here in the prologue of Hebrews we see that the author/preacher is making every effort to show that Jesus is the fullest and final message of God we could possibly have—if not the first impression of who God is then the final impression of who God is.

This is a major part of what Hebrews is all about, that Jesus really does show us what God is like (and if God is like Jesus, what's not to like about God?). Look at Jesus' life. Hear his teaching. See the way he shows loving mercy to people who everybody else thinks don't deserve it. Watch the way he makes sure children are included and feel important. Jesus embraces the people who the religious people call sinners and criticizes the ones sinners believe are religious.

Christ described as the imprint of God's very being is Hebrews' way of saying that Christ is God's way of making a true and lasting impression on the world. God knows impressions form quickly, and that they matter. But making the right impression matters most. And if Jesus is any example, getting it right in God's sight means authenticity and originality.

Anne: It's graduation season, so graduates across the country are hearing speeches about how they need to be themselves in the world. Be authentic to who they are, not who the world wants them to be.

Wake Forest University's Class of 2015 got some wise advice from Stephen Colbert, who'd recently agreed to host *The Late Show* after David Letterman's long tenure. Colbert pointed out that he's at a similar crossroads to the graduates:

> "It's time to say goodbye to the person we've become, who we've worked so hard to perfect, and to make some crucial decisions in becoming who we're going to be . . . From now on, you fill out your own report card . . . You are your own professor now."[5]

The thing is, as the graduates are nodding their heads to this, the parents are squirming in their seats thinking, "You just need to use this degree and get a job! Be successful! Be yourself, yes, but please, make a good impression."

Can we do both? Can we both be authentic to ourselves and make a good impression as we interview with a potential employer? Aren't we always, to some extent, acting in a way that we think that person wants us to act or saying what we think they want us to say?

When you think of people who make a good impression on you, it's probably because they say something or do something that resonates with you, how you think, how you act. So it seems that "making a good impression" is focused on the goal we're after—whether that be to land a job at the law firm or to get the guy to ask us out on a second date.

This thought may make us a bit uncomfortable; we like to think that we're not like that, that we're always 100% ourselves in any given situation. But actually, it may not be such a bad thing to not be fully ourselves when making a good impression. Especially when it comes to living as examples, or impressions, of Jesus in the world.

In this case, we absolutely do want to act in such a way that our lives resonate with Jesus' life. Though it may feel a bit false at first, the longer we do it, the more it becomes less of an impression and more of the imprint of God's very being on us.

Andrew: One of the only TV preachers I ever really liked was a guy from down in Austin, TX named Gerald Mann, who I once heard say: "I am not who you think I am; I am not who I think I am; I am who I think you think I am."

Totally convoluted, right? As adults, we can become masters at managing impressions. Some of this is fueled by the stories we tell ourselves about who we want to be or think we should be, or whom we want others to think we are. We learn to do this as we grow up because we live by the stories we tell ourselves.

But first there are all the stories that have been told to us about what it was like the day we were born or what our first words were or how we bit our preschool classmate when we were two. The stories we're told are the ones we eventually tell. These stories make impressions on our minds, and we learn about ourselves this way from an early age. But more importantly, we learn to tell stories.

Author and consultant Peter Block says that the stories of our past are heartfelt, but really they're all fiction. The only thing we know for sure is that we were born. We may know our parents and siblings and other family members and the roles they've played in our lives, but the meaning we take from our stories comes from us alone. In other words, the meaning of the story is *created*. Made up, in a way.[6]

And we do this every day in more common ways, don't we? We are such savvy storytellers that when our boss calls us to his office or we don't hear from our children for days on end or our spouse is giving us the silent treatment or a friend doesn't return our email in the time we think they should, we start filling in the blanks as to why. We begin jumping to conclusions without having all of the information in front of us. We start writing all sorts of stories, no matter how far from reality, leading us to stress and anxiety within ourselves and tension in our relationships because these stories are built on our assumptions about what's happening.

There is a wiser way than this—and we'd best take a page from Hebrews and absorb its wisdom that Jesus is not a false impression of God. Jesus is the imprint of God's very being. In other words, we can start at the top and consider again that Jesus is God's authentic stamp of approval that makes the authentic human impression of God's redeeming work in the world.

Speaking of making a good impression, Paul Durand-Ruel literally created the market for Impressionist paintings. He was a French art dealer, the first person to promote this emerging genre of artists. He supported them financially through the bad times and eventually found an audience that embraced their works as much as he did. An exhibition at the National Gallery in London a few years ago told his story alongside the works he loved and sold.

Not every painting in the show is a masterpiece. For example, the "Inventing Impressionism" catalogue describes Degas's "Peasant Girls Bathing in the Sea" (c. 1878) as "challenging." Some might call its "indistinct figures and smeary background a mess, unrecognizable to many as his work." The surprises in the exhibition come when the "fame, the big prices, the over-familiarity and the hype evaporate and viewers are able to see something extraordinary in the picture in front of them, much as Durand-Ruel was the first to do over a century ago."[7]

It makes me wonder what sorts of impressions of God you and I are making. Maybe not every moment is a masterpiece impression, and that's okay. But what if we can find those moments inside ourselves when all the over-familiarity and the hype of who we think we need to be or who we think someone else thinks we are can evaporate long enough for us to have an authentic connection—with God, with who we are, with each other.

The thing is, when it comes to making a good impression—just like the voices of the Hebrew prophets and the voice of Jesus in the Gospels—we are filling the world with words, words that can create life and order and understanding or words that can hurt and confuse and destroy.

For example we can say, "I am not worthy of love," or "I am God's beloved child." We can say, "I can't believe what you did," or "I forgive you." "I am not good enough for that," or "I have everything it takes to do this."

Anne: Just as the words we say about our own lives matter, so do the words we say about our life together. What impression are we giving of God in how we speak about our church? Are we saying words that build us up rather than words that break us down? Are we speaking truths about our church that are helpful instead of harmful? Are we perpetuating a narrative of change and loss and worry that's rooted in our past, or are we sharing the stories of energy, transformation, and spiritual growth that are happening all around us in our present?

How we speak inside these walls, the stories that we tell to one another about who we are or who we are not, shape us. We begin to believe them, whether they're true or not, and it doesn't take long before we're repeating them. What we say within about our church and within its walls shapes how the outside world sees us and experiences us—it's impossible to separate what we say in here from what people hear out there. We can try, but people will see through it.

In *The Scarlet Letter*, Nathanial Hawthorne writes, "No man, for any considerable period, can wear one face to himself and another to the multitude, without finally getting bewildered as to which may be the true."[8]

What is revealed in Jesus is at the heart of God. Said another way, Jesus reveals what's in the heart of God. What are we revealing about God's heart? How is God still speaking to the world through us?

This Sunday is Pentecost, the birthday of the church. It's a new year of life for us as a church family. And with every new beginning comes a chance to refresh and renew, shed old ways of doing things and live into new and better ways.

We hear echoes of the Acts 2 Pentecost story at the beginning of Hebrews 2: "God added his testimony by signs and wonders and various miracles, and by gifts of the Holy Spirit . . . " (v. 4).

We are the signs, wonders, miracles, and gifts of the Holy Spirit that God is using to speak to the world today. Since Pentecost, we are the ones that God is using to make impressions on the world. We can tell ourselves that what we say and what we do doesn't make that big of a difference. But that's simply not true.

We have the power to make a good impression.

Look around.

Even if Jesus is the fullest human impression of God, maybe he's not the final one.

Amen.

Notes

1. "Albert Camus," *Goodreads*, http://www.goodreads.com/author/show/957894.Albert_Camus (accessed May 24, 2015). Original: *The Stranger* (1942) and/or *Return to Tipasa* (1952).

2. Thomas G. Long, *Hebrews: Interpretation: A Bible Commentary for Teaching and Preaching* (Louisville: John Knox Press, 1997), 99–100.

3. Long, *Hebrews: Interpretation: A Bible Commentary for Teaching and Preaching*, 99–100.

4. Stephen Voorwinde, "Hebrews' Use of the Old Testament," *Vox Reformata* 73 (2008): 60, https://www.rtc.edu.au/RTC/media/Documents/Vox%20articles/Hebrews-Use-of-the-Old-Testament-SV-73-2008.pdf?ext=.pdf (accessed May 24, 2015).

5. Stephen Colbert, "You are Your Own Professor Now (Commencement Address to Wake Forest University Graduating Class of 2015)", *TIME*, May 11, 2015, http://time.com/3881609/snapchat-evan-spiegel-graduation-speech/ (accessed May 23, 2015).

6. Peter Block, *Community: The Structure of Belonging* (San Francisco: Berrett-Koehler, 2008), 44.

7. P.W., "Making the Impressionists," *The Economist* (2015), http://www.economist.com/durandruel (accessed May 22, 2015).

8. Nathanial Hawthorne, "The Minister in a Maze," in *The Scarlet Letter* (Boston: Ticknor and Fields, 1850).

Getting Down to Earth

Hebrews 2:5-18

When we say that someone is "down to earth," we mean that we can relate to them. Jesus is God's way of getting down to earth with us. He's relatable because he was fully himself, especially through his own suffering and struggles. Being this authentically down to earth with one another gives us hope for our own healing and the healing of others.

Andrew: [Monologue One] There's something that I've been meaning to say to you. I don't know why it has taken me so long to level with you about this. So, I'm just going to come out with it: I'm kind of a big deal. I've been biting my tongue for too long. It's hard to even know where to start, but I'll try. First of all, I'm pretty sure that nearly everyone who meets me believes that I'm quite intelligent and confident and decisive and charismatic. People love to hear me talk. I have expert opinions on just about any subject you can think of. Very few people feel like they can approach me because my good looks and my wisdom and my wit (and did I mention my intelligence?) are just too intimidating to people. So, I can understand why people might avoid me or feel like they can't relate to me, because I am uncommonly good at pretty much everything in my life. My work, for instance. Some say that I'm the best minister they've ever known, and I can see why. I write well. I speak well. I have a very comforting bedside manner when I visit people in the hospital. I am clearly special, and it's no wonder that people want to give me special treatment. And don't even get me started on what a fantastic father I am. I always know exactly what to say to my children. I always know what to do when my son starts flapping like a fish in the grocery store aisle wanting candy bars. I am President of the PTSA. I volunteer at the school all the time, because why would I rob everyone else of all my skills and gifts and abilities? I remind myself a lot of—oh—what's that Scripture in Hebrews? Oh yeah, I'm a "reflection of God's glory and the exact imprint of God's very being." (1:3).

Anne: What Andrew really means is . . .

Andrew: [Monologue Two] I'm just a normal guy, really. I don't want you to think more of me than what I am. And it's not that I'm especially intelligent or decisive or even overly confident. Not really. I am passionate about a few things, yes—I'm passionate about my work, about people, about my children. I do my best to share the gifts God has given me. And with God's help, I hope that I share those things generously and as well as I can. I don't know a whole lot. What I've learned is that I am a beloved child of God. I work hard; I care about people and their well-being; I love those God has entrusted me to love. I feel so lucky to have the job I have and that I to get to try to help people. And my goodness, I love being a dad, even though I'm not a perfect parent. (I mean, I let my kids eat dairy and watch television shows sometimes when I have to get work done. And, wow, they teach me so much more than I will ever teach them.) I certainly don't have all the answers when it comes to ministry or parenting or a lot of things, but I'm grateful for this life God has given me. I'm growing and I'm learning and I'm doing all I can to follow the spirit and teachings of Christ. And I'm grateful for all the grace that God gives me along the way.

Anne: So . . . which Andrew do you relate to better? The lofty, bragging Andrew or the humble, down-to-earth Andrew? I'm guessing you connect with the down-to-earth Andrew. Am I right? There's something about people being down to earth with us that draws us to them.

Last week, the writer of Hebrews introduced us to Jesus Christ, the "appointed heir of all things," (1:2), the "reflection of God's glory and the exact imprint of God's very being" (1:3), who "having become much superior to the angels" (1:4) is now reclining on his cushioned throne "at the right hand of the Majesty on high," (1:3). Okay, so maybe I threw in the "cushioned throne bit," but with all those lofty descriptors, I couldn't help myself. The Jesus of Hebrews 1 is impressive; he's clearly described as the exalted Son of God.

But much like the drastic difference in Andrew's monologues, in the span of a few verses, Jesus goes from way up here [motion high with one hand, toward the stained glass] to way down here [motion low with one hand, toward the congregation]. In chapter two, Hebrews brings Jesus down to earth. The author reminds us that Jesus "for a little while was made *lower* than the angels" (v. 9, emphasis mine). "He had to become like his brothers and sisters *in every respect* so that he might be a merciful and faithful high priest in the service of God" (v. 17, emphasis mine).

In other words, Jesus got up off his cushioned throne to mix and mingle with us common folk. And because he really did mix and mingle with us, he got mixed up in the same kinds of messes we do. Though Jesus was clearly special in God's sight, the world gave him no special treatment.

And why did Jesus come to earth? Verses 16-18 give us our answer. The contemporary paraphrase of the Bible by Eugene Peterson, *The Message*, reads:

> It's obvious, of course, that [Jesus] didn't go to all this trouble for angels. It was for people like us . . . That's why he had to enter into every detail of human life. Then, when he came before God as high priest to get rid of the people's sins, he would have already experienced it all himself— all the pain, all the testing—and would be able to help where help was needed. (2:16-18)

Now, while you and I might think it's great that Jesus came down to earth and experienced pain and death so he'd know what it feels like to struggle and suffer, people back then would have preferred for Jesus to stay in the sky with God. Or, if he did come to earth, they would have preferred for him to have defeated the systems of oppression that were still oppressing them. From their vantage point, the Messiah missed the mark and left them searching for meaning.

You see, the people who would have heard these words when Hebrews was first written were growing "ashamed of their association with a crucified Messiah."[1] In fact, as we'll see later in Hebrews, they're seriously thinking about "drawing back" from Jesus altogether (6:4-8; 10:32-39). And this isn't the kind of withdrawing that we saw Peter do on the night of Jesus' death, denying Jesus out of fear of being found guilty because he'd associated with Jesus. No, these believers were ashamed to be sporting the "Jesus brand" because not only was it unpopular, it seemed ridiculous, a poor product not worth a dime—not to mention a lifetime.

These people were beaten down by life, in part, because they knew Jesus, the one who was supposed to save them, was beaten down by life too. Jesus seemed to be no different than they were. In Hellenistic culture, gods are heroes who display their strength whenever they can, not rabbis who walk around and suffer like everyone else. Again, while it might be unfathomable to us, these early Christians are *withdrawing* from Jesus because he suffered rather than *drawing toward* to Jesus because he suffered. They don't yet have a developed theology to make sense of Jesus' death and they have no reason to believe that the world is different because of Jesus' life.

Modern readers can feel this way too. Preacher and professor Tom Long says, "Look at the world around us, and it hardly seems like the Son of God is running the show. From the hole in the ozone to the torn fabric of our society to the broken places in the human heart, all creation seems . . . chaotically out of control."[2] But this is the exact point the author of Hebrews is trying to make. Even in such a chaotic world, God doesn't stay separate and apart from the mess of our lives. Rather, God sent Jesus right into the heart of the messiness. And instead of being a sign of weakness, it's a sign of strength and power and even hope that God has a redemptive plan.

Verse 10 reads: "It was fitting that God . . . should make the pioneer of their salvation perfect through suffering" (2:10). Do you catch what this verse is saying? It's really important. It is in and through his suffering that Jesus is made perfect (or whole, we might say), not in and through a life of perfect living. Think about it: perfection, wholeness, and true wisdom—these are things we attain when we suffer.

In your own life, when have you grown the most in your faith or learned the most about God or yourself? When have you had the biggest "wisdom growth spurts"? I'm willing to bet that it had something to do with some difficult situation where you suffered in some way. When it comes to faith, we aren't great learners when things are going great. It's when we're suffering that we're open to transformation. And how could a God who has not personally known our suffering ever transform us? New Testament scholar Tom Wright illustrates this, saying,

> The author of Hebrews sees Jesus as the "pioneer": he is "the one who leads the way." Imagine an explorer cutting his way deep into the jungle. Nobody has been this way before; there are no paths, no trails, no signs that it's possible to go this way. Yet on he goes, forging his way through impossible terrain, until he reaches the goal. Once he's done that, others can follow.
>
> Explorers do that sort of thing for various reasons: fame or fortune, sheer curiosity. Jesus did it out of love. The jungle was the whole world of suffering, pain, sin and death. Nobody had ever gone through there

before and come out the other side. When he did it, he opened [a whole new] way in God's world . . .³

Jesus is the first one to introduce the fact that God suffers. God is not above suffering. By signing up to follow Jesus we're not signing up to suffer. We're going to suffer anyway; that's a fact of life. However, by following Jesus we're choosing to walk in the mud-caked footsteps of someone who understands our suffering, who has suffered before us and suffers alongside us, and who can help us through it. These footsteps belong to someone who's whacked through the mess of the jungle and made it out alive, who can show us the way through.

Ultimately, the point of Hebrews 2 is getting down to earth with God is possible because Jesus came down to earth with us. He's a messy Messiah, for sure. He stirred things up, he suffered, and he died. But that's why he's relatable. That's what makes him real. If you ask me, I'd rather Jesus be a "little lower than the angels" (v. 7) than be reclining on a cushioned throne up high "at the right hand of God" (1:3) any day!

Andrew: Yes, a messy Messiah. (You may have noticed that the first four letters of the word Messiah spell "mess.") Without Jesus, I don't really care about God, truth be told. If the glory of God is a human being fully alive, as St. Irenaeus once said, then I need a God who thinks enough of me as a human being to actually become one. Every human being wants to be truly alive and discover ways of living more truly and fully. Many people today (whether in the church or those who have nothing to do with church) talk about the importance of community and a place to be fully who they are. We're instinctively aware that there is something essential missing in life, something to look for beyond—or rather, in place of—the instant satisfactions proposed in today's consumption-oriented societies. We are all invited to share in a life of love. As Brother Roger, the late founder of the Taizé community in France, wrote on the day he died: "Yes, all God can do is give his love; that sums up the whole of the Gospel."⁴

Theological themes of perfection and suffering create threads of continuity through the book's thirteen chapters, creating a spiritual patch quilt of topics like testing, obedience, subjection, submission, covenant, sacrifice, and evil. It's established early in the book that Jesus, the pioneer of salvation, is perfected through suffering. Hear the text again: "It was fitting that God, for whom and through whom all things exist, in bringing many children to glory, should make the pioneer of their salvation perfect through sufferings" (2:10). We now ask the same question that the first-century believers likely asked: how do we follow Jesus in his sufferings?

Well, part of the answer is by being faithful stewards of our own suffering. And even before that, to accept suffering as endemic to human life. Poet David Whyte offers some spiritual alchemy about this that might help: "Once we have renounced the need to live without suffering, to be special, to be exempt from the losses and doubts that have afflicted all people since the beginning of time, we can see the difficulties of others without being afraid ourselves."[5]

And that's just what Hebrews is telling us; we can expect suffering in this life. Remember that Hebrews was written to a group of new Christians who were exhausted, and the writer of Hebrews is encouraging them not to give up or lose heart because their suffering and struggle could be the means by which they experience the full presence of Christ, the one who showed us the power of suffering love.

It's important to keep in mind that as the one Hebrews calls "the pioneer and perfecter of our faith" (12:2), Jesus did not go out looking for suffering. But he did embrace it when it came his way. And he didn't dramatize his own suffering either—Jesus was never a "woe is me" kind of person. He didn't live with the idea that the world was out to get him, even though it quite literally was.

The sort of suffering that Hebrews calls us to emulate is not suffering that we would go out and choose willingly. No. But what we learn of Jesus through our own suffering is what I might call "enlightened suffering"—a suffering that leads to life and not death. And the thing is, suffering that leads us to life and enlightenment is really hard to find on our own. We need to be around people who have been through difficult things and who have gained wisdom and insight to help lead us.

"God's love," states Hans Kung, "does not protect us against suffering, but it protects us in all suffering."[6]

And it is "in" our suffering that we are shaped by the pattern of Christ's suffering—not by the same type of suffering per se, but rather by the way we live in and through our suffering. Psychologists and spiritual mystics tell us that hurt people hurt people. As contemporary mystic and global spiritual teacher Richard Rohr has put it, "Pain that is not transformed is transferred."

Hebrews teaches us that Jesus is fully integrated into every detail of human experience. The fullest integration is that of his own pain and suffering, because the healing journey is always a journey of integration. To integrate suffering into our own self-understanding and identity is essential to being a person who is fully alive, even on those days when we might say, "You know, I'm trying my darndest to live like there is more light in God than darkness in me, but it's close!"

Every other Sunday morning, our congregation is invited to celebrate a twenty-minute service of contemplation and communion. Often, we draw from the liturgy of the Iona community in Scotland, which relates the full force of the meaning and redemptive intent of what we call brokenness or suffering. In the confessional prayer, the leader says aloud, "We confess to our brokenness; to the ways we wound our lives, the lives of others, and the life of the world." And the people respond, "May God forgive us, Christ renew us, and the Spirit enable us to grow in love." No matter how much like Humpty Dumpty we feel when our lives become scattered and shattered into pieces, confessing our brokenness around Christ's Table is a way of affirming that the broken body of Christ is still the body of Christ.

And, in a beautiful spiritual symmetry, immediately following celebrating Holy Communion, "we affirm God's goodness at the heart of humanity, planted more deeply than all that is wrong."

If Christ comes to us for no other reason, Christ reveals to us that our deepest beauty remains, no matter how covered up it is by things we have done or left undone, or by the things that have been done unto us. Deeper than the failings and wounds and heartbreaks of our lives, the beauty of the image of God is at the core of our being, planted more deeply than all that is wrong. And my goodness, there is all kinds of hope in that!

Anne: So how does all of this relate to our life together as a community as we seek to be transformed by the kind of hope that Hebrews offers us in this chapter? Well, to put it bluntly, we have to get emotionally undressed in front each other. We need to be willing to share our secrets and sufferings, because that's the only way to shed some light on them.

What if we thought of "sharing our suffering with others" as a spiritual discipline? We say that things like worship, prayer, reading Scripture, and serving the community bring us closer to God. Well, I venture to say that nothing brings us closer to God or to one another than being vulnerable enough to share what we're going through out loud with one another.

Jesus got down to earth with us and died the most vulnerable death possible. He hung naked on a cross. That's 100% failure by the world's standards. If we're to follow the example of Jesus, to emulate his life, then we need to share our suffering with one another, otherwise we're denying or avoiding one of the most important parts of his life, one of the key points of spiritual growth that God desires for us. There are no ifs, ands, or buts about it: if we're not being vulnerable and authentic with one another about the ways that we are suffering, then we're not experiencing the fullness of God in our lives.

All kinds of things keep us from this kind of intimate sharing. Fear of judgment and of what people will think, fear of looking weak or like you can't handle your "stuff." But imagine turning to the person next to you in the pew and saying, "You know what? I'm really struggling in my marriage. I feel like I'm not connecting to my husband anymore. I'm consumed with work, with the kids, with carpool to and from everything and everywhere. I want to rekindle that spark, but I have no idea how. He seems just as distant to me as I feel removed from him."

Or imagine that the next time you're in your Sunday school class and it's time to share prayer requests, that instead of saying, "Please pray for me, I have an appointment with my doctor to find out if the chemo is working," you say, "Please pray for me. I'm so scared. I have this sinking feeling that the chemo isn't working. I don't want to go to the doctor; I don't want to hear what she has to tell me. I try to put on a strong face for my family, but I'm crumbling on the inside. I don't want to die. I want to see my kids get married. I want to be there for my wife. I thought I was doing okay, handling this cancer thing, but I'm really not."

Do you think that if you shared these kind of deep feelings with someone here that they'd laugh at you or blow you off or think that you are weaker or lesser than? There's no way. I imagine they'd view your openness and reaching out as an act of strength, not as a weakness or as a plea from someone who is, heaven forbid, "needy." We're all needy, are we not? So let's drop the illusion that we don't need one another. We do. It's part of our created nature.

Yes, this kind of sharing feels uncomfortable and extremely vulnerable and very unnatural at first, but doesn't it feel way more real than just saying, "Oh, I'm fine" when people ask how you are or what's going on? Our culture equates strength and power with the absence of suffering, or, at the very least, never admitting to anyone that you're suffering. But the culture of Christ is way more down to earth. It recognizes that suffering is part of life, and it highlights suffering as one of the greatest ways of deepening spiritual growth and gaining wisdom. Is suffering fun? Of course not. But it's real. And it makes for a strong faith.

The author of Hebrews encourages the people of his day by giving meaning to Jesus' suffering. He helps them understand why Jesus came down to earth to suffer and die and why that doesn't make him any less of a Messiah; in fact, it makes him more of one. Hebrews works to persuade us that Jesus' suffering is one of the greatest gifts he has to offer us.

Likewise, if we're not being vulnerable with one another and seeking the wisdom that is stored in each other's hearts and minds from years of our vast and varied experiences, then we're not taking advantage of the greatest gift that the church has to offer. I asked you to do this last week, and I'm asking you again this week: look around. Really look around at the people in this sanctuary.

Think about all of the wisdom borne of suffering that is in this room right now. Are we taking full advantage of this wealth of wisdom for our own spiritual growth? There's no better place than the church to practice getting down to earth with our faith, our failures, and all our hopes for the future. So, as we get at the heart of Hebrews, let's not forget to get into our own hearts as well.

Amen.

Notes

1. Luke Timothy Johnson, *Hebrews: A Commentary* (Louisville: Westminster John Knox Press, 2006), 98.

2. Thomas G. Long, *Hebrews: Interpretation: A Bible Commentary for Teaching and Preaching* (Louisville: John Knox Press, 1997), 37.

3. Tom Wright, *Hebrews for Everyone* (Louisville: Westminster John Knox Press, 2004), 19-20.

4. Brother Roger, "Brother Roger's Unfinished Letter," August 16, 2005, http://www.taize.fr/en_article2964.html (accessed May 30, 2015).

5. David Whyte, *The Three Marriages: Reimaging Work, Self, and Relationship* (New York: Penguin Publishing, 2009), 234.

6. Hans Küng, *On Being a Christian* (Garden City, NY: Doubleday & Co., 1976), 436.

Lighten Up: It Doesn't Have to be This Way

Hebrews 3

Following Jesus means living life with and for others, not just for ourselves. The upside of this life journey is that we have partners to learn from along the way. The downside is that, in living with our differences of personality, theology, and habits, we can lose focus and fail to keep the main thing the main thing. It doesn't take much to develop a hardened heart. Hopefully it doesn't take much to soften one and lighten up either. The Christian community is at its best when we're in it to give of ourselves rather than to get something for ourselves.

Anne: This week, the congregation is at the heart of Hebrews. After two heavy chapters of lofty Christology and suffering theology, the preacher lightens up a bit and, for the first time, addresses his audience directly, with affection and as equals, saying, "Therefore, brothers and sisters, holy partners in a heavenly calling . . ." (v. 1).

This is a pivotal shift. It's as if you've been sitting across the table from someone, listening to them talk *about* you, and then they turn, look you in the eye, and begin to talk *to* you. The preacher gets personal with his people, explaining why Jesus matters to them and what difference he makes in their lives. Remember, this is important because the persecuted Hebrews were struggling to see how Jesus mattered to them at all. This whole letter, or sermon, is meant to encourage them in their faith and re-energize their commitment to Christ.

The best way the preacher knows how to do this is by comparing Jesus to one of their local heroes: Moses. Moses was to the people of Hebrews as Adoniram and Ann Judson are to American Baptists, as John Elway is to the Broncos franchise and fans, and as Triple Crown winner American Pharoah is to thoroughbred horse racing enthusiasts.[1] The people held Moses up on a pedestal, so by invoking his name and reputation, he knows he'll catch their attention.

Now when he says that "Jesus is worthy of more glory than Moses" (3:3), he's not bashing Moses in order to build up Jesus. "The intent is not to cast a shadow on Moses but to shine a light on Jesus."[2] The comparison is meant to build on Moses's reputation as a faithful leader by saying that someone even greater than he is here in the person of Jesus.

Next, the preacher uses the metaphor of a house to compare Jesus and Moses. And by "house" he means a living community, not a building. In the first century, a household would be large and diverse, with several generations of adults, kids, and servants. One of our favorite commentaries says, "Hebrews invites us to imagine the whole history of God's people as one vast family, a spacious household embracing many generations—from Abraham, [Sarah, and Hagar all the way to you and me today]. So, where do Moses and Jesus fit into this grand household of God? [Well, to follow the metaphor,] Moses was faithful in the house as a servant; Jesus was faithful over the house as a Son, in charge of the house as the heir" (vv. 5-6).[3] Notice that they're both faithful and spoken highly of, but they have different roles and missions. Just like we all do.

And we, the people, are actually pulled into this metaphor in a quick but crucial twist in verse 6: "Christ . . . was faithful over God's house . . . and we are his house if we hold firm the confidence and the pride that belong to hope," (v. 6). In this one verse, the people become God's house, "brothers and sisters" (v. 1) in Christ, and are magnified in God's household—that is, in all of history. In hearing this message, a huge responsibility shifts onto their shoulders. They are "holy partners in a heavenly calling" (v. 1). And the preacher is banking on this sense of responsibility to make them feel special enough to want to give Jesus another shot.

Frank Lloyd Wright, a well-known architect and author, once said, "When designing a house, you have to ask what the people want to live in, but you must also keep an eye on what they want to live for."[4]

As Tom Long explains,

> If the Hebrews' congregation is to be faithful, if they are to truly be the house of God, enduring to the end, their faith must be anchored in that which is beyond the turmoil of their present circumstances. If they

trust only what they can see, they are lost, adrift. If, however, they hold firmly to and live for that which they have heard, that which can only be known in hope, then they can truly be the church with 'confidence' and even 'pride.'"[5]

And then in another very personal move, the faith of this congregation is compared to the faith (or lack thereof) of their ancestors, the Israelites. The writer of the letter to the Hebrews essentially says to his community what the Southern writer Flannery O'Connor said over two thousand years later in a letter to her friend: "The meaning of redemption is precisely that we do not have to be our history . . . ."[6]

Andrew: The hope of this redemption (that we don't have to be defined solely by our history), is put precisely in today's text: "Therefore, as the Holy Spirit says, 'Today, if you hear his voice, do not harden your hearts as in the rebellion, as on the day of testing in the wilderness, where your ancestors put me to the test, though they had seen my works for forty years'" (vv. 7-10a).

The past and present are connected here because the people of God are still the people of God, no matter what century we live in.

Remember, too, that the preacher of Hebrews is writing to a discouraged congregation. They have "drooping hands" and "weak knees" (12:12). Their memories of hardship, struggle, and affliction are still fresh (10:32-34). We don't know exactly what this congregation had gone through, but what's true is that they are wandering in their own wilderness just like their ancestors. The difference, though, between *then* and *now* for this congregation is the difference between hardening their hearts and being what Hebrews calls "partners of Christ," holding their "first confidence firm to the end" (3:14).

In other words, they are not doomed to repeat a failed history. They can learn from the past without being controlled by it. The ancestors who wandered in the wilderness for forty years lost hope and lost heart. They became people who cried about their crisis. They became chronic complainers about how in the world God could have led them out of Egypt only to have dragged them into the wilderness for forty years.

You see, then as now, the human tendency is to abandon hope when hardship comes, when life isn't turning out the way we think it should or when God doesn't seem as actively involved in the world or our lives in ways that make sense to us. And the wisdom of Hebrews sees right through all the crying and complaining and the bickering, all the moaning and groaning that went along with Israel's rebellion. Hebrews essentially says, "It doesn't have to be this way for you!" And in good biblical fashion, the preacher of Hebrews quotes Scripture—Psalm 95 to be exact. This is where we hear,

> O come, let us worship and bow down, let us kneel before the LORD, our Maker! For he is our God, and we are the people of his pasture, and the sheep of his hand. O that today you would listen to his voice! Do not harden your hearts, as at Meribah, as on the day at Massah in the wilderness, when your ancestors tested me, and put me to the proof, though they had seen my work. For forty years I loathed that generation and said, "They are a people whose hearts go astray, and they do not regard my ways." (Psalm 95:6-10)

Imagine this being read aloud in a worship service to a congregation who would have regularly heard Psalm 95 in synagogue services. It's saying, "Pay attention! Take heed. Don't let your hearts be hardened. Israel's failure to be faithful to God then does not have to be your story now. It can be different for you. So be bold. Be confident in Christ. Hold on to hope. Even in the midst of your frustration and struggle and suffering, God's never-ending and never-changing love is still very much alive and at work for your good."

It is as if the preacher of Hebrews is saying, "Lighten up so you can live up to your full potential as partners of Christ." Keep hope alive by encouraging each other, so that your hearts won't harden and turn away from the living God. Don't let discouragement take you over, because it distracts you from your holy calling to keep the main thing the main thing. St. Francis puts it this way, "We have been called to heal wounds, to unite what has fallen apart, and to bring home any who have lost their way."[7]

Hebrews is a congregation that has lost its way. The writer is calling them to remember what brought them together in the first place, to reclaim their first confidence as "partners of Christ." Isn't it easy for us as a congregation to lose our way when we are distracted by our doubts and fears and hurt and struggle? Our own biases and opinions can sometimes have a similar effect. We, too, can abandon hope. Discouragement can take us over. Our collective hearts can harden, and we can become people who just go through the church motions without having much emotion about the church. By "emotion," I mean passion or compassion; what the heart of the church is really about in being partners with Christ. The temptations of the children of Israel and the children of the church of Hebrews are our temptations, too. Motivations can cause us to be in the church *for ourselves* rather than being in to *give something of ourselves.*

Hebrews reminds us afresh that it doesn't have to be this way for us. Yes, the people in the wilderness fell away and lost hope. And people can fall away from the church and lose hope because they are upset or angry or jaded. Some people don't ever make it close to anything that looks like church because of the stereotypes or reputations that they learned about the church from afar.

Fear can also hold us back from doing our best work and being our best selves as a community. Author Christian Piatt has helped me think more about this idea:

> Too often, our actions in church are governed principally by a response to what we fear might happen, rather than faithfully discerning what God is calling us to do. We assume that the only way to tell if we're being faithful is if the church buildings are full and the budgets are met. But this mandate is nowhere to be found in the Bible. To the degree that our institutions can serve our call to live out the gospel, more power to those who are stewards of them. But when the fear of losing them becomes the focus of our work together, they are the idols we've come to worship more than God.[8]

I think this is a fear that we all would do well to lose. In the good and bad times of life in a community like ours, it can be easy to see ourselves as "managers of a religious organization." To think like this and live like this and lead like this is spiritually detrimental according to Hebrews. Rather, we are "holy partners in a heavenly calling" (3:1). And we forget this to our peril.

When we forget this, and maybe some of us in this room today have actually forgotten this, we can become like the congregation in Hebrews—disheartened, tired, uninspired, discouraged about church, and distracted from keeping the main thing the main thing. We live in a "Twittery" world of chronic noise and often shallow communication about things that aren't always very important. So, we are conditioned for distractions in ways that can lead us away from the main thing Christ came to show us: love.

What are some ways we might need to lighten up? Are we distracted by things that keep us from making the "main thing the main thing"?

Occasions arise when I sense I need to check myself about my role and responsibilities, not just as a minister on a church staff but as a Christian. I ask questions like, "How often do we use the word 'Council'[9] versus the word 'Christ'?" The truth is that we aren't just mangers of a religious institution. We aren't just here to count nickels and noses. We are partners with Christ. And that identity must inform and guide everything we do as a spiritual community. It's how we see our purpose and ourselves as a church when we keep the "main thing the main thing."

Anne: And so, if Christian community is at its best when we're in it to give of ourselves rather than to get something for ourselves, then the same holds true in our personal relationships. Just as the physical arteries in our hearts don't harden over night, but do so gradually as we continually eat a fried, high-cholesterol, unhealthy diet, so too do the spiritual and emotional arteries in our hearts harden through gradual and continual dining on unhealthy perspectives and attitudes like negativity, criticism, and comparison.

When it comes to our friendships and marriages, our children and our partners, our hearts begin to harden the minute we start to doubt their love for us, compare their actions to ours, mistrust their feelings, or question their motivations:

"I always load the dishwasher; she just leaves her dishes in the sink."

"He comes home from work, flops on the couch, and turns on the TV, saying he's exhausted. Doesn't he understand that I'm exhausted too? Just getting the kids to bed is a monumental task, not to mention running them around all day and getting homework done . . . ."

"Why does she never say 'I love you' anymore? I say it every day and she says it back, but she's never the first one to say it."

This habit of comparison starts at a young age. Without us even knowing it, our hearts are hardening when we say things like, "Mom, it's not fair. She has more ice cream than me." It builds through our teenage years: "Why does he get to stay out as late as I do? When I was his age, you made me be home by ten o'clock." When we reach adulthood, before it hits our closest relationships, our friendships feed this comparison behavior too: "Last year I gave her a gift for her birthday, but she only gave me a card for mine, so this year I'm only going to give her a card." And, of course, it finds its way into the office too: "He doesn't work as hard as I do but he gets paid more than me. He's always late and he never seems prepared."

The reality is, we never really know the full truth of another person—even of our closest partner. So whenever we compare ourselves to them, it's bound to just harden our own hearts rather than heal any kind of rift in our relationship.

So how do we lighten up and soften our hearts? Well, it takes practice. The spiritual practice of lightening up might begin with this question: "How much does this really matter to me in the grand scheme of life? What is this costing me in time, energy, and blood pressure?" Everything we do has a cost, good and bad. If we choose to focus on one thing, it takes away our energy directed toward everything else. So, we need to make sure what we are focusing on is the main thing.

This is what the preacher of Hebrews is hoping to get across to his people: that if they cling to Christ and commit to him, then their future will be different than their past. Their complaints and concerns will become less important to them as they commit to loving as he loved, serving as he served.

This is essentially what Jesus did in his ministry with people. He came to simplify the law: Love God; love others (Lk 10:27). Why do we make these two things so difficult? Jesus gives us so many examples of how, when push comes to shove, it's really not that hard to put love first. He looked at the law of the day, looked at the needs of the person in front of him, and made decisions: "This person is hurting. It is the Sabbath and I'm not supposed to work today. But this person is hurting. What's more important? Enforcing this law or relieving this person's pain?" With Jesus, the person won every time. Lightening up is an action borne of a changed attitude; it's something we can all do. We are all capable of making this shift in our lives.

Because here's the thing: we are "holy partners in a heavenly calling" (3:1). We are in it *with* each other, so we might as well be in it *for* each other. And no one shows us how to do this better than Jesus. In fact, this is the very reason he came to earth, to remind us that life is about loving God and loving others.

We need this reminder. We need it so much, we keep coming to the Lord's Table again and again. At the Table, we are reminded that Jesus Christ is the source of our hope. We are reminded of the history of our faith and all that brought us here—all of the mistakes, miracles, and mundane moments. And because we always come to the Table with others, we are reminded that we are siblings in Christ, "holy partners in a heavenly calling"

(v. 1). And to remember these three things is to remember the things that really matter in life, the things that are worth carrying around.

If you are carrying burdens and concerns that have nothing to do with these three things, then lighten your load. Leave all that other stuff with God. It really doesn't have to be so hard. There's another way: the Way. And the Table leads us there.[10]

Amen.

Notes

1. The racehorse American Pharoah won the Triple Crown (the first such winner since 1978) the day before we preached this sermon.

2. Thomas G. Long, *Hebrews: Interpretation: A Bible Commentary for Teaching and Preaching* (Louisville: John Knox Press, 1997), 49.

3. Ibid, 50-51.

4. Ibid, 52.

5. Ibid, 52.

6. Censor Librorum, "Flannery O'Connor's Catholic Lesbian Friend" *Nihil Obstat*, March 12, 2009, http://nihilobstat.info/2009/03/12/flannery-oconnors-catholic-lesbian-friend/ (accessed June 6, 2015).

7. Wendy Murray, "Remembering St. Francis of Assisi," Patheos, October 4, 2013.

8. Christian Piatt, "5 Things That Are Holding Christianity Back," http://www.huffingtonpost.com/christian-piatt/five-things-that-are-hold_b_3983052.html?ncid=edlinkusaolp00000003 (accessed June 6, 2015).

9. Calvary Baptist's Council is the primary leadership body of the congregation, most closely related to the Board of a nonprofit organization, with some functions of the Deacon body of many Baptist congregations.

10. The end of the sermon leads directly to the Lord's Table, beginning the celebration of Communion.

Reclaiming Rest[1]

Hebrews 4:1-13

Too often we are lured into living life in the fast lane. Do you need a break from work, worry, stress, or life, but feel like you can't make the time for it? We easily break the commandment to "remember the sabbath day, and keep it holy" (Ex 20:8), compromising our own physical, emotional, and psychological health in doing so. Even more than a commandment, God gives us an open invitation to rest. The practice of rest is a way to fulfill our hope to more closely connect with God, our work, our loved ones, and ourselves.

Andrew: " . . . I did make a conscious decision, a long time ago, to choose time over money, since I've always understood that the best investment of my limited time on earth was to spend it with people I love. I suppose it's possible I'll lie on my deathbed regretting that I didn't work harder and say everything I had to say, but I think what I'll really wish is that I could have one more beer with Chris, another long talk with Megan, one last good hard laugh with Boyd. Life is too short to be busy."

So begins a *New York Times* essay from writer and cartoonist Tim Kreider. The essay laments what Kreider calls "The Busy Trap," the constant bee swarm of busyness that pushes us to do more, be more, have more while we chronically complain about our lack of free time. Kreider calls himself "the laziest ambitious person I know," but he praises something different than laziness. He praises idleness.

Here's what I think he means: Idleness is not just a vacation, an indulgence, or a vice. It is as indispensable to the brain as vitamin D is to the body, and deprived of it we suffer a mental affliction as severe as rickets. The space and quiet that idleness provides is a necessary condition for standing back from life and seeing the whole, for making unexpected connections and waiting for the wild summer lightning strikes of inspiration—it is, paradoxically, necessary to getting any work done.[2]

It's as if taking time to do nothing helps us figure out what we should be doing the rest of the time. Being busy is not a moral accomplishment any more than being exhausted is a sign of physical health. In fact, as we'll learn more today through Hebrews, busyness can actually be a sign of a threatening spiritual condition that can lead to spiritual symptoms like rebellion, disobedience, and hard hearts. Social symptoms can arise from the same source: We drive too fast. We eat in the car. Our lives are just crammed full, and it leaves us running on empty.[3]

Think about how we feel and how we behave when we are worn out, exhausted, and depleted. We get grumpy. We get mean. We get irritable. Our fuse is shortened. We start saying things we don't mean. We start doing things we would never think to do. We throw things around like a four year old who doesn't get their way. We may not throw food or toys, but we can throw out names and insults and any chance of being a calm, peaceful person, someone at rest. It's like driving a car when you're falling asleep. Things can careen out of control, and we can do damage to ourselves and others.

Through all of this busy madness, I wonder: why do we work so hard? Where does all of this glorification of busyness (or even spiritualization of busyness) come from? Why do we keep from "making every effort to enter into God's rest"? (v. 11a).

Well, ironically, the way we think about work and being busy and the importance we place on these things has an origin in Protestant Christianity. A professor at the University of Georgia, Roger Hill, spoke about this in a 2012 interview with American Public Media. He says that in the time of Hebrews, work was seen as a curse. Even with the Greeks, they had pretty bad attitudes about work. And this continued into the medieval period. But then what came along in the sixteenth century was the Protestant Reformation. People began to be able to choose what work they wanted to do. Plus, religious people wanted evidence that they were part of the elect—people whom God had chosen to go to heaven—and one of the ways people judged that was by their perceived success in life. Thus was born what we now know as "the Protestant work ethic." People came to see their identities as tied to a search to be successful, a quest to secure economic well-being.[4]

Now, consider this: people in the United States work more hours every year than people in any other advanced country in the world except for

South Korea and Japan. (In Japanese there's a specific word for "dying at your desk" or "death from overwork": *karōshi.*)[5]

Many of us are exhausted. We feel stretched. We're sleep-deprived. We're overworked and under-nourished, and we're not always sure what to do about it. When nobody around us is defining what "enough" is, our bodies will. Sometimes lack of stillness can lead to illness. When we're physically spent and we have nothing more to give, sometimes an illness is the only way we can get rest and relief. Sometimes it's the only way we don't feel guilty that we're not doing more. Sometimes illness isn't enough to avoid guilt.

Our cultural addiction to busyness is an American idol that has made sacred idleness culturally passé. We need help to remember to rest. Why? Because we're so bad at it.

Anne: And we aren't the only ones who are bad at it. The Hebrews were too, although the rest promised in Hebrews is much different than simply a good night's sleep, a shorter work week, and more vacation time.

Rest, it turns out, is an enduring gift from God that is both beyond time and within time. This chapter begins with the hopeful assurance to the Hebrews that "the promise of entering [God's] rest is still open" (v. 1). You may think it odd that the preacher here is speaking of rest as if it were a door that could open and close. But these people were exhausted and persecuted, and they were just warned with a rant about how their ancestors did not listen to God as they wandered in the wilderness and developed hardened hearts—which is why, according to Psalm 95, their ancestors did not enter God's rest.

With this grim history at the forefront of their minds, it would be a welcome word that the Hebrews' ability to rest was not just a future fantasy—it's actually feasible for them in the present. They can enter God's rest here and now, provided they make the effort by listening to God, obeying Christ, and keeping their hearts open to faith.

There are three key words in this passage: "today," "rest," and "effort." Let's start with the word "today." "Today" has three meanings, the simplest one being the most literal: this calendar date. But "today" also means the present tense of the Hebrews' human experience—which is one of waning faith, exhaustion, and increasing persecution. "Today" means that even in the midst of such chaotic and unrestful circumstances, rest is available. And finally, "today" also carries what Tom Long calls "the sense of urgent time, the critical moment in terms of faith . . . the *kairos*, the 'eternal now.'"[6]

When someone tells you to do something today, there's an urgency that has nothing to do with the actual calendar date, but has everything to do with the fact that it needs to be done immediately. Such is the nature of this writer's urgency for rest.

Which leads us to our second key term, "rest." Many Old Testament passages talk about rest, but the main one the preacher of Hebrews draws on is Psalm 95. That psalm was widely used in the early church "as a call and guide to worship," so the congregation would have been familiar with it.[7] Psalm 95 speaks of "rest" as the quality of being with God, which presumably means worshipping God in the Temple.[8] Then, the preacher uses Genesis 2 to expand upon the meaning of rest: "And God rested on the seventh day from all his works" (4:4; Gen 2:1-3).

Rest is not only a gift from God that has been around since the beginning of time, rest is an action of God, critical to the completion of creation itself. In other words, for God to create, God must rest. In the same way, for us to create and be in the world—we must rest too. And, God deems rest so important that God sets it down as a commandment to the Israelite people: "Remember the Sabbath day and keep it holy" (Ex 20:8).

The origin of "rest" in the act of Creation means that this Sabbath celebration transcends the rest forfeited by the Exodus generation and anyone after who refused to rest. "Rest" remains available "today" to everyone who believes (Heb 4:4).[9] In other words, even though their ancestors didn't accept this gift of rest in its full form, the gift remains. And it remains because the giver of the gift is God, Our Creator, not some king or ruler, leader, boss, teacher, or parent. It transcends time because it has a divine origin, not a human one.

There is a sense that "rest" also refers to a future end time when creation is finally restored and all people are fully redeemed. This future eternity of rest gives context and meaning to our present need for it. Tom Long describes this relationship between the past, present, and future meanings of "rest" well:

> "Rest" is not just a concept applying to the beginning and the end; it is also a quality of Christian life in the middle of time, a calm assurance of participating in the will of God (4:3). Even now, as Christians struggle to be faithful in the midst of ambiguity and turmoil, the promise is that all of this counts, that their faithful actions are being gathered into God's everlasting purposes. God uses the prayers and deeds of ordinary people of faith to redeem the whole of creation.[10]

We can "rest" here and now knowing that in the end God's kin-dom will come and every action we do in the name of Christ, no matter how small or large, is part of the fulfillment of God's kin-dom here on earth.

Just as we take part in the future possibility of God's eternal rest, we also take part in rest today. And it requires "effort," which is our third key word. Verse 11 reads: "Let us therefore make every effort to enter that rest, so that no one may fall through such disobedience as [the Israelites']." It seems ironic to think of rest as requiring effort, but I think we all know that to truly rest takes intentional work and commitment and, let's be honest, it doesn't come naturally to us. We are restless.

The preacher takes a whole chapter to emphasize rest because of just how crucial it is. Besides being an act of God on the seventh day of creation and a commandment from God brought down from Mt. Sinai by the hands of Moses, rest is critical to our ability to sustain faith for the long haul. As St. Augustine prayed to God: "You have made us for yourself, and our hearts are restless until they find rest in you."[11]

Andrew: St. Augustine's prayer is our prayer too. Deep down, our restless hearts tell us that we are indeed made by and for God, and intended to live our lives with and toward God. If rest is truly a crucial part of fulfilling God's promise of peace, what is it that keeps us from accepting God's gift?

Notice that this is the only commandment that begins with the word "remember": Remember the Sabbath. Keep it holy.

Also notice that a significant portion of the sermon of Hebrews is devoted to helping the people remember the critical importance of rest and encouraging them to make every effort to enter into it.

As Anne said, it seems ironic that we should have to make an "effort" to enter into such a rest, but even Jesus knew it required intention and planning. Remember Jesus' generous invitation in the Gospel of Mark to "Come away to a deserted place all by yourselves and rest a while" (Mark 6:31).

Jesus' invitation as well as the preacher of Hebrews telling the people that "the promise of entering his rest is still open" suggests we should step back and see what God saw at creation, that everything "was very good" (Gen 1:31).

Apparently, even Jesus knows that we need extra help to stop and taste and see the good gifts of God. Now, there's no sign that any of the disciples had health-related problems. Mark doesn't report that John was having chest pains or that Matthew was battling anxiety or that Peter had high blood pressure. If they did, though, Jesus could probably read the warning signs. Maybe he could see the fatigue in their faces. He never went to medical school, but the Gospel of Mark says there were times that Jesus ran the only clinic in town. Hordes of sick people needed his treatment. This time, Jesus prescribes rest for his depleted disciples. They had become the spiritual equivalent of starving chefs. Sick people needed healing, hungry people needed food, anxious people needed peace, tired people needed rest, but the disciples are people too. There were limits to what they could do. And the people of Hebrews had bumped up against their limits to such a degree that the disciples were losing heart and losing hope. It seems they had forgotten that God's redemption did not start with them and it would not end with them. They desperately needed to accept that God's rest was part of the design, not only for Creation but also for creating and re-creating the life God was calling them to live right in the middle of their real-life circumstances.

I often think the gross neglect of our limits most keeps us from rest. We only have a finite amount of time and the ways we use or don't use it, spend or don't spend it, says as much about what we're doing as it does about who we are. We need to respect our limits and guard them from ourselves and others. Too little respect for our limits can lead us to confuse or even forget what *really* matters from what only *seems* to matter. And we need Sabbath and rest to figure these things out.

Remembering the Sabbath is not about keeping a rule. After all, Jesus says, "The sabbath was made for humankind, and not humankind for the sabbath" (Mk 2:27).

Essayist Ahad Ha'am wrote, "More than the Jews have kept Shabbat, Shabbat has kept the Jews."[12] That is to say, the Sabbath is not merely about treating a day of the week like it's holy. Keeping the Sabbath is about keeping us whole. Wayne Muller, in his book *Sabbath: Finding Rest, Renewal, and Delight in Our Busy Lives*, describes how the Sabbath can either be a single day or a way to cultivate the practice of Sabbath rest. He says, "when we consecrate time to listen to the still, small voices, we remember the root of inner wisdom that makes work fruitful. We remember from where we are most deeply nourished, and see more clearly the shape and texture of the people and things before us."[13]

Speaking of a still, small voice (from a small body): just this week, I was driving my children to the babysitter's house. It was a perfect Denver day. After days and days of rain, the sky was as clear and clean as if the rain had washed it blue all over again.

I told my 6-year-old daughter, "You know, sweetheart, I wish that we could spend the whole afternoon at the swimming pool, but Daddy has to go to work." Addison said, "Dad, work is boring." And I said, "Well, sometimes it is. But a lot of times it's not. Sometimes it can even be fun." She asked me when it was fun, and I answered that it's fun when I feel like my work is really making a difference and when I feel like I am really helping people.

Then she asked the question at the heart of the whole conversation, "Daddy, do you like *us* better or your work better?" I said that "There is nothing in this world that I like better than you." She smiled and seemed to find comfort in that. I found rest and renewal in the words of this 6-year-old spiritual teacher of mine; rest from all of my mental to-do's that morning; rest that puts into perspective what's really important in life.

She is worldly wise, you understand, but she's mostly spiritually wise. After we read Scripture on Sunday mornings, we say "For the Word of God in Scripture, for the Word of God among us, for the Word of God within us." Well, this was the "Word of God among us" part that day, right from the lips of my little girl. As Hebrews says about the Word of God being "sharper than any two-edged sword, piercing until it divides soul from spirit" (4:12), it was a Word of God that divided for me what *really* matters from what only *seems* to matter.

Anne: Speaking of what really matters and what doesn't, isn't it quite absurd that even though God needed rest and rested on the seventh day of Creation and instituted it as one of the Top 10 things critical to the covenantal relationship, we think *we* don't need it? God commanded it alongside such things as having no other gods, not coveting, not killing, and not committing adultery, but we modern, industrialized, technological people think that we are above rest, that it's not an important priority. Who do we think we are?

I joke with some of you about this, but it seems that all of you who are retired are busier now than when you were working. You make retirement look tiring! Although, I guess the difference is, retirement is full of those things that give you life, those things you choose to do, things that you didn't have time to do while you were working, so it doesn't feel so much like work. You're volunteering at church and in the community, caring for your grandkids, exercising, and traveling. This is the difference in finding rest in what you are doing and in doing things until you're so exhausted you're forced to rest.

But most of us, well, we break this commandment of rest and of "keeping the Sabbath holy" all the time. And we don't hold each other accountable for it. Nobody seems to like to claim that they are a "rested person." We like to claim things like: "Sorry, I am so busy at work—I have a lot of deadlines and important deals—I don't have time to do that." How many of us long to be able to say, "Sure, I can do that because I am really rested right now"? (By the way, has anyone ever noticed that "deadline" has the word "dead" in it?)

Or we say things like, "My kids are working hard to make sure they get scholarships to good schools: they're in honors classes, school clubs, varsity sports, orchestra, and are active in youth group." How many of us long to say instead, "My kids are rested and creative and will do well in life because they understand balance and that being centered and rooted in God is more crucial to their faith and health than having their lives revolve around their classes and activities. Getting close to Christ is more important than getting into college. The two aren't mutually exclusive, but Christ comes first."

And if we don't long to say these things, why? Probably because no one, the Church included, is asking us to think this way! A hectic life is just part of our culture, which doesn't make it right, but it does make it seem normal. By contrast, "keeping Sabbath is a decidedly different way of living: it is deeply counter-cultural. It is living out an intentional witness, a resistance to the way things are. When we live differently, we live with God."[14]

And this is precisely the preacher of Hebrews' point. By not keeping Sabbath, by not keeping faith, the people are not really living with God. We can't just live on any terms we want to and tell ourselves we're living as God wants us to. Being children of the Protestant Reformation and shaped by the Protestant work ethic doesn't excuse us. As Christians, we are supposed to be different and live differently.

Hebrews is clear that we can't have a partnership with God apart from rest—the spiritually renewing kind of rest that is called Sabbath. So, how do we find this? What will it take for us to really reclaim rest and become, once again, "holy partners in a heavenly calling" (3:1)?

First, we should eliminate any idea in our heads that we have to prove our worth to God, to others, and to ourselves. We are worthy of rest because we are beloved children of God. Period. End of discussion.

Second, we must realize that Sabbath rest is not the opposite of doing. Sabbath rest is not an all-or-nothing thing that has to happen on one day.

(Although, isn't it glorious when it does!) We can find rest in our everyday living if we have a restful perspective and incorporate moments of renewal in our schedules. In the same way that God rested after creating and then kept on creating, we too find rest in the midst of our work. Luke Timothy Johnson writes, "[People] who accept this gift [of Sabbath rest] 'cease from their works not in the sense that they cease human effort, but in the sense that, like God, their works are no longer a striving to fill a need, but [are rather a sharing] in [the] outpouring of [God's] abundant life."[15] Jesus did say, "I came that they might have life, and have it abundantly" (Jn 10:10).

In his book *The Sabbath*, Abraham Joshua Heschel says, "There is a realm of time where the goal is not to have but to be, not to own but to give, not to control but to share, not to subdue but to be in accord. Life goes wrong when the control of space, the acquisition of things . . . becomes our sole concern."[16] Instead, "the higher goal of spiritual living is not to amass a wealth of information [or things], but to face sacred moments."[17]

Facing sacred moments is what Sabbath is all about: taking time to drink in the beauty of the created world around us, the love of the life-giving relationships that hold us up, and taking time to recognize and name these things as "God." And we need to give others the permission and encouragement they need to do this as well. When someone says to you, "I can't seem to find time to exercise or spend time with the kids. I'm so tired, I'm working 70 hours a week," it is not okay to say, "Yeah, I know. Join the club. That's life, right?" No. According to God, that's not life. God created life and sustains our lives, so God should know.

Maya Angelou, a seemingly endless fount of wisdom, wrote,

> Every person needs to take one day away. A day in which one consciously separates the past from the future. Jobs, family, employers, and friends can exist one day without any one of us, and if our egos permit us to confess, they could exist eternally in our absence. Each person deserves a day away in which no problems are confronted, no solutions searched for. Each of us needs to withdraw from the cares which will not withdraw from us.[18]

This is Sabbath rest. The cares of the world won't leave us, so we have to leave them. It takes practice. Pastor Andy Stanley gives us four practical ways to think about creating Sabbath space in our lives:[19]

1. What do I need to delete from my calendar? (What really matters? And what only seems to matter?)
2. What do I need to add to my schedule? (Have I created white space in my calendar?)
3. What do I need more of in my schedule? (What is life-giving to me?)
4. What do I need less of in my life? (What is draining me?)

Think on these four questions this week. Your spiritual health depends on it. And our spiritual health as a community of faith depends on it too. Here's a confession: your pastors are part of this too. We haven't always done a good job of setting a Sabbath example. But we need your help, just as much (or more!) as you need ours.

Who wants an exhausted and grumpy church? Let's be a life-giving church. Let's become "holy partners in a heavenly calling" (3:1) by being healthy partners in a heavenly calling with God and one another. Let's reclaim rest. Let's counter our culture and celebrate Sabbath.

To put it simply: let's give ourselves permission to say no to some things in order that we can say yes to God in all things.

Amen.

Notes

1. Tim Kreider, "The 'Busy' Trap," *New York Times*, June 30, 2012, http://opinionator.blogs.nytimes.com/2012/06/30/the-busy-trap/?_r=0 (accessed June 13, 2015).

2. Ibid.

3. Dean Schabner, "Americans Work More Than Anyone," *ABC News Online*, May 1, 2015, http://abcnews.go.com/US/story?id=93364 (accessed June 12, 2015).

4. Roger Hill, *Where did the American work ethic come from?* http://www.marketplace.org/topics/life/where-did-american-work-ethic-come (accessed June 11, 2015).

5. Brigid Schulte, "5 reasons why you shouldn't work too hard," *The Washington Post*, February 21, 2014, http://www.washingtonpost.com/blogs/she-the-people/wp/2014/02/21/5-things-you-get-from-working-too-hard/, (accessed June 11, 2015).

6. Thomas G. Long, *Hebrews: Interpretation: A Bible Commentary for Teaching and Preaching* (Louisville: John Knox Press, 1997), 55.

7. Derek Kidner, *Psalms 73-150* (Downers Grove, IL: InterVarsity, 1975), 343.

8. Randall C. Gleason, "The Old Testament Background of Rest in Hebrews 3:7-4:11," *Bibliotheca Sacra* 157 (July–September 2000), 296.

9. Gleason, *The Old Testament Background of Rest*, 299.

10. Long, *Hebrews*, 59.

11. Saint Augustine of Hippo. *Confessions*, trans. Henry Chadwick (New York: Oxford University Press, 1991), 3.

12. Rabbi Shawn Zevit, "More than Jews have kept Shabbat, Shabbat has kept the Jews," February 4, 2016, https://mishkan.org/rabbishawn/blog/more-than-jews-have-kept-shabbat-shabbat-has-kept-the-jews (accessed February 11, 2020).

13. Wayne Muller, *Sabbath: Finding Rest, Renewal, and Delight in Our Busy Lives* (New York: Bantam, 1999), 5.

14. Donna Schaper, *Sabbath Keeping* (Boston, MA: Cowley Publications, 1999), 19.

15. Luke Timothy Johnson, *Hebrews: A Commentary* (Louisville: Westminster John Knox Press, 2006), 130.

16. Abraham Joshua Heschel, *The Sabbath* (New York: Farrar, Straus, and Giroux, 1951), 3.

17. Heschel, *Sabbath*, 6.

18. Maya Angelou, *Wouldn't Take Nothing for My Journey Now* (New York: Random House, Inc., 1993), 126.

19. Andy Stanley, "Breathing Room: Time," *North Point Community Church*, January 13, 2013, http://northpoint.org/messages/breathing-room/time (accessed June 14, 2015).

Not Afraid to Ask for Help

Hebrews 4:14–5:10

Asking for help is one of the hardest things for us to do. Why is this? Is it because we don't want to be a burden to people? Are we afraid people won't think we're competent or capable? If Jesus, the Son of God himself, was vulnerable enough to offer prayers and to express his needs with "loud cries and tears" (5:7), then why can't we? If we can learn to ask for help, we will change our lives for good and for good.

Anne: We're five chapters into this text and five weeks into this sermon series, so it should be crystal clear by now that Christ is at the heart of Hebrews. Jesus is the one raising hope in the lives of the Hebrew people, who because of persecution, suffering, and even apathy, have a lackluster hold on the faith that they once so strongly professed. The author of Hebrews is holding Jesus up to these people as their "diamond in the rough," not because he is hidden away somewhere, waiting to be found like a long-lost treasure, but because their blinders and limiting perspectives keep them from seeing him.

A diamond has many facets, or faces. And what allows you to see the multidimensional beauty of a diamond? Light. It may be a simplistic metaphor, but it is as if the preacher is holding up Jesus to them like a diamond and saying, "As a people on the verge of having the same hardened hearts as your ancestors, not only have you lost sight of Jesus (this diamond, this great gift)—but you have yet to even discover just how many facets of himself he can show you. Look carefully! There are so many more aspects of Jesus to discover and understand. And once you do, you'll realize that the light shining through them all is the hope that you are so longing for in your lives. You can't experience the complete wholeness of the hope Jesus has to offer unless you see and experience all of these aspects."

I know not all of you have been here every week, so let's do a brief review of the facets of Jesus we've discovered so far in this book. We first met Jesus in Hebrews 1 as an exalted figure sitting at the right hand of God, the reflection of God's glory and the imprint of God's very being. In Hebrews 2, we met Jesus as the flesh and blood God, a suffering pioneer who came to earth as one of us and therefore can empathize with us. Then in Hebrews 3, we saw Jesus as God's son, faithful heir of God's household (meaning, of all human history). Jesus is held in higher esteem than even Moses, the great hero of their ancestors' faith. And now in chapters 4 and 5, we see the intersection of these three dimensions of Jesus in a whole new facet, that of the great high priest. Jesus comes from God to be with us as a human. Because he understands our lives and our suffering, he has the greatest authenticity of experience and authority to face God on our behalf. It is because Jesus sits at the right hand of God in heaven and sits at the right elbows of his disciples and friends breaking bread on earth that he is the great high priest, the great mediator, between God and humanity.

And that's what a high priest is—a mediator. Our biblical knowledge may not cover the Levitical priesthood in depth, so allow me to give us all a refresher. In essence, "the task of a priest is to approach God on behalf of the people, to gather what the people bring—their offerings, their prayers, the symbols of their repentance, their cares, their deepest needs—and to take these offerings into the very presence of God. The priest . . . faces in two directions . . . toward God on behalf of humanity [and] toward humanity on behalf of God."[1]

When the people needed help and forgiveness from God, the priest took their confessions and sacrifices to God for them, along with his own. And he returned with a blessing from God for the people, a reminder of their salvation, their wholeness. Here are some other things to know about priests. God appointed them; the priesthood wasn't made up of volunteers. It was a very important role with guaranteed job security. After all, the people were never going to stop sinning, so the priests were never going to stop sacrificing. But then there was a very pastoral dimension to the priesthood too. The priest would hear the deep secrets and confessions of the people, and he could sympathize with them as a fellow imperfect human who also messed up from time to time.[2]

So why does the preacher of Hebrews call Jesus the great high priest? Well, first of all, it's a term and office that the Hebrew people could relate to and understand. However, there are some clear distinctions. God designates Jesus from the beginning (Jesus was not appointed), and because of Jesus' eternal nature, there is an eternal nature to the message of wholeness and forgiveness and salvation that he brings to the people. In other words, he's a "forever" priest—not just for their lifetime, but for all of time. In this chapter, the most important part of Jesus being the great high priest for the Hebrew people is his understanding of their suffering. Jesus is a great pastor. He's able to empathize and sympathize with them, bringing their sins and hurts to God alongside his own cries and laments. And the best thing about Jesus as high priest is that his offering, his sacrifice, is once and for all.

Will the people keep sinning and needing to confess and restore right relationship with God and others? Yes, of course. But the gift of forgiveness and the blessing of wholeness and salvation is already theirs. Jesus doesn't have to keep bringing them new blessings of salvation from God because he himself is the source of salvation itself.[3] He is the one in whom the world and all the people in it are made whole. His very life and his love are the blessing. "And the Word became flesh and lived among us . . . " (John 1:14).

So the main facet, or face, of Jesus that the preacher is sharing with his people today is this: Jesus is their great high priest. And instead of carrying burnt offerings or animal sacrifices to God, through his life and death, Jesus carries the "whole of our human condition to God—our need, our distress, our pain, our infirmities, our hunger for justice, and our cries for peace."[4] He takes all of this and boldly places it before God. "It is striking that, while several statements are made about [Jesus'] learning, his being tested, his suffering, and his faithfulness," the strongest image in in the chapter "is that of Jesus in fervent and agonizing prayer."[5]

The image of Jesus praying with loud cries and tears, appealing to the One who is able to save him from death, brings to mind Jesus in Gethsemane. The late, great preacher Fred Craddock wrote, "That Jesus' prayers were heard and yet he still suffered poses no theological problem; rather, it locates Jesus more firmly among his brothers and sisters whose experiences are precisely the same. The posture of Jesus is that of one facing death . . . like the rest of us, he cries out to God in the face of the immediate prospect of death."[6]

The reason Jesus is so great a high priest is because he actually asked God for help, crying out on his own behalf as well as on behalf of his people. This pastoral high priest dimension of Jesus is so important for the Hebrews to understand—and for us to understand too. Jesus is the great high priest, the ultimate mediator. He is the connecting bridge between God and humanity because he approaches humanity with humility, coming down to earth to suffer alongside us. Also, he bridges humanity and God because he approaches God with humility, crying out to God and lamenting the suffering of humanity. He gets both sides, so much so that humanity and God can no longer be referred to as two different sides, but rather as one—joined together by Jesus the Christ.

Listen again to what a gift this is in Hebrews 4:14-16 from *The Message*: "Now that we know what we have—Jesus, this great High Priest with ready access to God—let's not let it slip through our fingers. We don't have a priest who is out of touch with our reality. He's been through weakness and testing, experienced it all . . . . So let's walk right up to him and get what he is so ready to give. Take the mercy, accept the help."

"Accept the help." I was going to preach about how even though it's inherent in Jesus himself and an essential aspect of being a Christian, "asking for help" seems to be the cardinal sin in our American culture. We champion independence over dependence, individual success over communal progress. I was going to refer to an article that talked about the assumptions we hold about asking for help that keep us from doing so: not doing something on our own is a sign of weakness, allowing someone to help us means we lose control of the situation, asking for help burdens someone just as busy as me, accepting support from someone means I have to return the favor sometime and help them. And then there's the idea that I'm the only one who can do it right, and it's quicker for me to do this than to teach someone else how.[7]

These assumptions are fascinating, and they are worth exploring because they really are opposite of the behaviors and teachings of Christ. Indeed, we have a long way to go in our spiritual formation of being counter-cultural in this way. But I'll save that message for another day because, as the week unfolded, I felt a very different message in my heart arising from this text. Today's passage contains a message of healing and reconciliation that comes when we actually allow Jesus to be our high priest, our mediator. It's a message of hope that can be ours if, and only if, we actually believe and start acting like we're the living, whole body of Christ.

When my Baptist colleague and pastor of New York's Riverside Church, Rev. Amy Butler, responded to the murders of nine people at Mother Emanuel AME church in Charleston, South Carolina, her comments felt like they could have come from my own heart. So I share them with you today:

> Words are insufficient to capture the depth of grief, anger, and despair many of us have felt as we heard the news of this violent act of terrorism fueled by a shameful legacy of racism in our country. Our prayers and our hearts go out to the families of the nine precious lives lost, to the congregation of Emanuel AME Church, and to the city of Charleston, SC. Tragedies such as these confront us with hard questions.
>
> As people of faith, how can we speak words of peace and reconciliation when even our houses of worship cannot provide sanctuary from the violence and hatred in our world? How can we proclaim all lives are cherished and beloved by God when our brothers and sisters are targeted for the color of their skin? How can we hope for a culture of peace and justice when we do not even have the courage to limit the use of deadly weapons in our society?
>
> Our lack of resolve, our collective failure, has created this litany of tragedies. Still, it is in these moments of despair that we need each other most. We need our churches and communities to provide comfort and to call us to action with the deep conviction of our faith—a faith that gives us the courage to speak words of hope into a culture of death, a faith that compels us to work for justice and God's peaceable kingdom on earth as in heaven, a faith that assures us love and not hatred will win in the end.[8]

With all of this on my mind and heart, I kept wondering, What does Jesus being our great high priest have to teach us about how we live and move and have our being as people of faith in this world?

To see Jesus as our high priest is to see Jesus as a connecting point, a mediator, a bridge between humanity and God, and Lord knows we need that in our country right now. As an American people, we have sinned and fallen short of our created and intended potential, and we must seek forgiveness from God. But even more than forgiveness from God, we who are white must seek forgiveness from people of color as we work for racial justice for all.

The thing about Jesus as high priest, about him being the mediator and bridge from us to God, is that because he's fully human he understands us in full and fully represents us to God. And, because he's fully divine, he also understands God and fully represents God and the fullness of God's love to us. What would it be like for us to allow the life and love of Jesus to be our high priest, our mediator and connecting point between races in our country?

What would it be like to see one another through Jesus' eyes, in the fullness of all humanity and as beloved children of God? What would it be like for white people to fully see people of color as God sees them? For us to sit down across a table from one another and see ourselves fully represented and heard before God and one another through Christ? What would it be like to see ourselves as the person across the table from us? To believe that we are them and they are us?

What would it be like to realize that we are not the broken people that our world accepts and even creates, but that in God's kin-dom, we are one body in Christ, equal before God and one another? Can we have the courage to let Christ mediate our racial biases and prejudices and propel our country from conversations about race to actions of reparations and restorative justice?

Hebrews 5:7 says, "Jesus cried out in pain and wept in sorrow as he offered up priestly prayers to God" (*The Message*). What does Jesus teach us here? Jesus shows us that as long as humanity is suffering and sinning—as long as there is pain and death and racism and hatred and terrorism and mental illness and political infighting to strip others of their rights—there must be loud cries pouring out of our mouths and prayers soaked with our tears.

Why else do we need Jesus to be our high priest and mediator? Because we do not know how to talk to one another across party lines or race lines or religious lines. We do not know how to sit down as communities and put language around systemic racism. Instead, we live in the illusion that we can face these deep faults in our society on our own—with our guns and our politics no less. But we can't do this. Why? Our hearts are hardened with denial; our vision is blinded by our own needs. And as we wander in this wilderness, we're killing ourselves and others, literally. Haven't we proven, time and again, that whatever we're doing isn't working?

This is why we need Jesus as our interpreter across seemingly impossible divides. We need him as our Prince of Peace who came and suffered and sacrificed for all people, not just people of certain colors or races or economic means or sexual orientations or gender identities or religions. Jesus is the great priest for all people, for all time. No exceptions. And if this is the Jesus in whom we profess our faith and the Jesus we know that we need in our lives and in our world, then why aren't we following him? Why do things our own way? Why aren't we looking to Jesus for help?

Why do we see Jesus' peaceful ways and still think violence is the answer? Why do we see Jesus sitting down with people of differing perspectives and still think it's best to only hang out with and talk to people who think and believe and look like us? How can we hear Jesus say that loving God and loving others are the two most important commandments, then keep on loving ourselves more and more?

Why don't we white people ask for help? I think we're afraid we might be perceived as racist. But guess what? Systemic racism is the air we breathe, the water we swim in. What can we expect when our country was founded on land stolen from indigenous peoples we massacred and built by the labor of the brown and Black bodies that we enslaved? We who are white must acknowledge this reality and how it shaped our worldview and culture. So let's admit it, seek forgiveness, educate ourselves, and take action. Let's look to our great high priest—our mediator of all mediators—to see what to do, how to get help. Let's cry out to God, lament the dead, pray for the survivors, and let's mourn the racism and the prejudice that that is built into the very fabric of our country. It won't die because white people thrive on keeping it alive. We benefit, even when we aren't aware of it, and we're terrified of losing that advantage.

When we've reckoned with our past and how it continues to affect our present, and when we've committed to the work of actively being antiracist, let's also realize that wholeness and salvation have already come in Christ. Though we are living in a Good Friday world, we are resurrection Christians. We are the risen body of Christ, alive and at work in the world. When one of us is broken, we all feel something broken inside of us. Our AME brothers and sisters are suffering, as are all people of color in our country. How are we helping? We are crying out to God in prayer, yes, but what else? How are we changing our systems and our behaviors once and for all?

As people under the Levitical priesthood, we have to offer sacrifice after sacrifice with prayer after prayer for death after death and sin after sin. How do we move to living as people under Jesus' priesthood, believing in the power of his love and life? How do we truly soften our hearts, believing that his suffering and sacrifice allows us to approach God and one another with boldness, with mercy, and with grace?

Well, one thing is for sure. We can't be afraid to ask for help. We have no choice at this point. We must ask for help from our great high priest and we must be a source of help for our siblings in Christ. And you know what? Our brown and Black siblings aren't afraid to ask for help. They welcome the help of white allies and white churches. Where are we?

In an article for the Huffington Post titled "7 Ways To Be A White Ally For Charleston And The Black Community," Aaron Barksdale offers a few things white people need to keep in mind as we seek to help, and not hurt, the situation:

1. **Don't reinforce the mental illness or "loner" narrative.** Racism is not a mental health condition and should not be used to explain away the shooter's actions, as if they occurred in a vacuum.
2. **Learn about the history of the AME.** This attack is both an assault on the Black community and a symbolic landmark. Emmanuel AME's roots date back before the Civil War with a congregation officially founded in 1816 by both slaves and free Black people.
3. **Reject the notion that the attack was part of a war on Christianity.** Emmanuel AME was chosen because of its Black population.
4. **Dispel the myth that more guns solve problems.** The NRA argues that if one or more of the church members had had a gun, then the victims could have shot back at Roof, and might have survived. Let's be clear: placing guns in spiritual sanctuaries, places that are supposed to be safe, will not eradicate our country's racism or save more lives than racism takes.
5. **Remember the names of the victims.** Honor the lives that were lost in this tragedy: Depayne Middleton-Doctor, Cynthia Hurd, Susie Jackson, Ethel Lance, Clementa Pinckney, Tywanza Sanders, Daniel Simmons, Sharonda Coleman-Singleton, and Myra Thompson.
6. **Understand the history connected to terrorism on Black churches.** Over 100 churches have been targets of terrorist acts since the Civil Rights Era. Given the important role churches have played in Black history, these hate crimes strike at the heart of Black communities.
7. **Connect to the Black Lives Matter movement.** Realize that this tragedy is part of a larger system that devalues Black lives. Read more. Pay attention. Have compassion. Speak up.[9]

White people's silence not only fails to help African Americans and other people of color, but actively causes harm. Real and deadly harm. Will we act like the Christ that we say we follow, crying out to God with bold laments? Will we be agents of reconciliation, bridges of hope, and mediators of our broken humanity to one another and to God? Will we listen to people of color first, finding ways to partner with them without talking over them?

Iva Carruthers, general secretary of the Samuel DeWitt Proctor Conference, an interdenominational faith group focused on social justice issues, spoke this week at a luncheon for the New Baptist Covenant. Her prophetic words hit at the heart of our call as Christians:

> The Charleston church massacre is not a problem of gun violence or even of racism. Rather, it uncovers a spiritual sickness afflicting the American soul. The challenge in America is one of "soul lockdown," a spiritual and moral malady blinding the nation to the systemic racism, white entitlement and other entrenched attitudes that inspire events like Wednesday's mass shooting in South Carolina.
>
> [This] soul lockdown limits the movement and perception of truth and confines the outward flow of the breath of God. Well-known slogans that have come from incidents of law enforcement violence, such as "I can't breathe," "no justice, no peace" and "black lives matter," often function as metaphors of the condition. . . .
>
> All of us are on soul lockdown and none of us can truly breathe . . . the prescription for soul lockdown includes immersion into a process of reconciliation that addresses deep, systemic forms of racism and white entitlement. Those must be replaced with the ancient African notion of Ubuntu: "my humanity is bound up in yours." It will take a "serum of truth" to enable Americans to see that African Americans have been war crime victims in their own nation and that the United States was built on the back of their free labor. That truth must include confession, reparations and reconciliation."[10]

While those things are clear, Carruthers said one uncertainty remains, whether the church will lead or follow in this process?[11]

Gary Simpson, pastor of Concord Baptist Church in Brooklyn, N.Y. agreed saying, "Whatever form the action takes, there must be action . . . I think we've got to tell the truth, and the truth is painful . . . the church must take the lead in the movement . . . It's a noble call, but it is our call—'thy kingdom come,' right?"[12]

The reason Jesus is at the heart of Hebrews is because the preacher can't find enough ways to remind his people of who Jesus is in their lives and what his life and death means for the world and for all people. We need just as many reminders of who Jesus is and the power he holds as the Hebrew people did. We, too, are a disheartened people. But I firmly believe that Jesus is the one raising hope in our lives.

We must let Jesus, our high priest, be the bridge between our broken humanity and between our broken hearts and the heart of God. May we be unafraid to ask for help as we seek to be a part of the hard work of reconciliation in our country, for it's in admitting that we need help and that "our way" can only lead to failure that the true healing begins.

Lord, have mercy . . .

Amen.

Notes

1. Thomas G. Long, *Hebrews: Interpretation: A Bible Commentary for Teaching and Preaching* (Louisville: John Knox Press, 1997), 65.

2. Long, *Hebrews*, 67-69.

3. Long, *Hebrews*, 67.

4. Long, *Hebrews*, 65.

5. Fred B. Craddock, "The Letter to the Hebrews: Introduction, Commentary, and Reflections" *The New Interpreter's Bible Volume XII*, (Nashville, TN: Abingdon Press, 1998), 64.

6. Craddock, *The Letter to the Hebrews*, 62.

7. Lorie Corcuera, "5 Mistaken Beliefs About Asking for Help" *Inc.com*, September 10, 2014, http://www.inc.com/lorie-corcuera/become-a-better-leader-by-asking-for-help.html (accessed June 14, 2015).

8. Amy Butler, "A Statement from Pastor Amy on the #CharlestonMassacre," *The Riverside Church in the City of New York Facebook Page*, June 18, 2015, https://www.facebook.com/RiversideNY/posts/10153423269806133?-fref=nf&pnref=story (accessed June 21, 2015).

9. Aaron Barksdale, "7 Ways To Be A White Ally For Charleston And The Black Community," *Huffington Post: Black Voices*, June 19, 2015 (accessed

June 21, 2015), http://www.huffingtonpost.com/2015/06/19/white-ally-charleston-black_n_7623758.html.

10. Jeff Brumley, "'Soul lockdown' afflicts nation, inspires tragedies like S.C. church shooting, activist says," *Baptist News Global*, June 19, 2015, https://baptistnews.com/article/soul-lockdown-afflicts-nation-inspires-tragedies-like-sc-church-shooting-activist-says/#.XNwz0NNKhTY (accessed June 21, 2015).

11. Ibid.

12. Ibid.

Preschool or PhD: Where Are You in the School of Faith?

Hebrews 5:11–6:12

When it comes to faith, we all start in different places and progress at different paces. We say "faith is a journey" all the time, but doesn't the destination make a difference? To what degree is faith important in your life? Is it important enough for you to keep learning and growing beyond what's convenient or comfortable?

With the demands of our lives, it would be easy to say about faith, "Let's just keep it simple and easy." But if we choose to remain sluggish in our spiritual development, we forfeit the hope of ever becoming fully mature followers of Jesus, of making a lasting impact in our world, or even just living a life with meaning and purpose.

At its best, church schools us in the Way of Christ, cultivating an intelligence of the mind and heart.

Andrew: Preschool or PhD: where are you in the school of faith? This searing question lies at the heart of our Hebrews text today. Is the question direct? Yes. Is it personal? Yes. Is the whole premise a little snobby? Maybe. Is it a little insulting to suggest that some believers may be babies while others are fully grown adults? This is the preacher of Hebrews' point today.

I've seen all sorts of t-shirts lately that say, "Faith is a journey, not a guilt trip." I like that. And even more than faith not being a guilt trip, it can be a good trip. But before it's a good trip, the preacher has to pester his congregation a little bit.

The author (or preacher) of Hebrews does not mince words about the matter at hand: ". . . we have much to say that is hard to explain, since you have become dull in understanding" (v. 11).

You'd think he would start with a kinder, gentler strategy. After all this time, the people ought to be teachers by now. In a sense, the ones who ought to be PhD's in Christ have regressed to being a bunch of preschoolers drinking milk from their spiritual sippy cups. They now need to re-learn the basic elements of faith. They could be advanced enough to be feasting on "solid food" as the text says, "But solid food is for the mature, for those whose faculties have been trained by practice to distinguish good from evil" (v. 14). They aren't progressing enough in their spiritual education to be the informed and transformed witnesses to Christ they need to be. So instead, they're being told (or scolded may be more like it) that they need to enroll in a remedial course to re-learn what they ought to already know. Their moral aptitude and their attitudes about ethics ought to be more fully formed, but they're not. So Hebrews uses these familiar images of milk and solid food not as culinary categories, but as categories of educational development. They are struggling in their course with Christ, and the preacher of Hebrews is telling them with unmistakable directness that they are going to be "faith flunkies" if they don't grow up and get beyond the basics.

Getting beyond the basics means becoming spiritually mature through spiritual practices of growth and staying open-minded enough to keep learning and embrace what Hebrews calls "perfection" through the redeeming grace of Christ (6:1). Now that word "perfection" can trip us up, so permit me to explain it briefly.

Up until now in Hebrews, the word "perfect" or "perfection" has been limited to talking about Jesus. Remember last week, when Anne talked about Christ as the high priest and pointed out the different facets of what Christ as the high priest could mean then and now? She said, "Jesus is the great high priest, the ultimate mediator. He is the connecting bridge between God and humanity because he approaches humanity with humility, coming down to earth to suffer alongside us. Also, he bridges humanity and God because he approaches God with humility, crying out to God and lamenting the suffering of humanity. He gets both sides, so much so that humanity and God can no longer be referred to as two different sides, but rather as one—joined together by Jesus the Christ." And so, in chapter 5 we get at the theological heart of Hebrews with Jesus' role as high priest. The preacher says of Jesus, "Although he was a Son, he learned obedience through what he suffered; and having been made perfect, he became the source of eternal salvation for all who obey him, having been designated by God a high priest according to the order of Melchizedek" (5:8-10).

This is high-level stuff. Now, the preacher of Hebrews shifts the language of perfection from Jesus to the ones that he's just called a bunch of babies, saying, "Therefore let us go on toward perfection . . ." (6:1a). Like a dedicated professor, he is prodding these would-be faith flunkies who are "dull in understanding" (5:11) to go from being immature infants to imitators of Christ.

Rather than being lazy slackers at the back of the class, this "professor of progress" in Hebrews is using his powers of persuasion (or the art of insult) to motivate this congregation to get to the head of the class again, to keep growing, keep maturing, and keep cultivating the kind of love shown in its fullness in Christ. Going deeper, we see that we aren't to be satisfied with a superficial, shallow, easy life of faith. There are truths that you can only learn in the depths. Don't be immature toddlers, be imitators of the Master teacher, Christ.

As New Testament scholar Tom Long has said, "A Christian who faithfully imitates Jesus is like a pianist who plays Mozart well. If a critic observes that the pianist 'played the concerto to perfection,' it is, of course, an achievement of a different order than that of Mozart himself. The 'perfection' of the performer depends upon that of the composer. So it is with the Christian life."[1]

I'm fond of saying that "practice doesn't make perfect; practice makes progress." And this is what the professor of progress in Hebrews is trying to get across to his dimwitted students in his own confrontational style.

The idea is to keep practicing the faith. It is a long journey, for faith is not a lightning flash or a one-time event. Practicing our faith is something you can't learn to do right the first time and then be done with it. The perfection comes with repetition. Faith, to be perfected, must be practiced.

The 11th-century Christian philosopher St. Anselm's motto was, "faith seeking understanding." It means something like "an active love of God seeking a deeper knowledge of God."[2]

Some of us love that. We love gaining understanding. In fact, I think all of us love it—it's just that many of us do not like putting much effort into it.

Or if we do, we want to know how long it's going to take before we get the answers we want or have the enlightenment we seek. It reminds me of a story I've heard in one place or another about the martial arts student who went to his teacher and said earnestly, "I am devoted to studying your teachings and your ways. How long will it take me to master it?"

The teacher's reply was casual: "Ten years."

Impatiently, the student answered, "But I want to master it faster than that. I will work very hard. I will practice every day, ten or more hours a day if I have to. How long will it take then?"

The teacher thought for a moment and answered, "Well, in that case, twenty years."

We may end up all the more oblivious to the divine nature that is all around us for having tried to master it as fast as we can. It's easy for our western minds to want to keep faith as easy and simple as possible and turn it into how God wants us to have a happy, purposeful life in seven easy steps. Biblical Christianity isn't that way. What Hebrews gives us is richer and more complex.

Up until today's text, the preacher of Hebrews has believed that his congregation could handle complexity—maybe even be comfortable with complexity. Consider how Hebrews talks in such complex language about who Christ is and what his life and death and resurrection mean for them and for the world.

But somewhere along the way, they got a little lazy. They became spiritually lethargic. They shrunk back from being the bold witnesses for Christ they once were. They stopped encouraging one another. But they have the opportunity to begin again, for God "will not overlook your work and the love that you showed for his sake in serving the saints, as you still do" (6:10).

Hebrews again hoists a flag of hope, clearly signaling that the congregation could once again know the depth and power of being imitators of Christ, embracing afresh the fullness of faith they once knew.

And yes, this fullness of faith will lead to them being more fully formed followers of Christ. The thing is, if it's the filet mignon of faith that you want, this is it. Chew it carefully and well. Let it take time to digest. It is the meat of the "word of righteousness" (5:13) that you need; not just the milk.

This is the difference between being infants and being grown-ups, spiritually speaking. Grown-up believers have way more to chew on, so to speak, than those who have just been born into the life of faith. And those mature believers know that adult Christianity is not a problem to be solved or a fictional ignorance to explain away. Even more, purely analytic intelligence may be powerless to receive the full depth and breadth of the mature faith that characterizes the whole of Hebrews.

The maturation of faith is more than just gaining more knowledge, as the deep well of our faith reveals. Virtually all of the Christian mystics have basically defined spiritual maturity as the mind descending into the heart.[3] And this is of a different kind of intelligence altogether. It is more to do with transformation than information. It is more to do with an intelligence of the heart than being some born-again brainiac. To gain the wisdom of the way of Christ is a kind of beautiful secret hidden in plain sight. Really, it's about intimacy more than just intellect.

My favorite spiritual teacher Richard Rohr says that when we get right down to it, the beautiful secret hidden in plain sight is that "an infinite God seeks and desires intimacy with the human soul. Once you experience such intimacy, only the intimate language of lovers describes what's going on for you: mystery, tenderness, singularity, specialness, changing the rules 'for me,' nakedness, risk, ecstasy, incessant longing, and, of course also, suffering."[4]

This is all a language of the heart that Jesus knew so much about through his relationship with the one he called Abba. Jesus' name shows God's willingness to be vulnerable and the human face of God's love.[5] And love, if we read Hebrews through the life and story and teaching of Jesus, is both the source and the goal of the Christian spiritual life.

Such a language of love is the heart and soul of intimate relationships. Relationships that have any depth to them whatsoever are usually ones in which secrets and desires are shared. The most vulnerable parts of us are usually shared in the presence of sorrow, failure, or need, when we feel entirely safe in the arms of someone else's love.

I think this is why the preacher of Hebrews can speak in such an open and candid manner with his congregation. Beyond the insults at the beginning of today's text (calling them babies and dull in understanding) and the threats and fear-inducing language in the middle of today's text (saying it is impossible to restore to repentance those who were once enlightened and then have fallen away), we finally get to the clincher: "Even though we speak in this way, beloved, we are confident of better things in your case, things that belong to salvation" (6:9).

After the spiritual regression of the congregation; after many of them had fallen away after threats and persecution and having their property taken away, Hebrews hoists the flag of hope again. The "stern professor" tone turns to a "loving parent" tone. Upon hearing these words, the congregation must have felt entirely safe in the arms of love. They had been playfully taunted and even chastened by their preacher as a way to motivate them to progress in their faith. They had been confronted with hard truths, and they ultimately were told that they were "beloved" (6:9).

This is what happened with the congregation in Hebrews. And this is what happens in our congregation, too.

A sacred space emerges in our souls where we can feel the full force of that word: beloved. In this created space, we can feel beloved by our community and by God, no matter where we are on the journey to a PhD in Christian love. Here, we feel most fully human, living alongside our failures and follies and flaws. At our best, we're all seeking a PhD in the school of love. Church serves as the place where we are all human enough to feel and share love.

There is no time like the present to work toward a gutsy, grace-filled, grown-up faith. More than ever, the world needs some grown-up Christians.

The grace to be respectful of one another amid differences is gritty and gutsy, grounding us in Christ's genuine love. This gutsy grace allows us to become something greater than we once were. While laws, lands, and nations will change, God's law of love will never change. St. Augustine said, "in essentials unity, in non-essentials liberty, in all things love." A mature church can be a haven for those diminished by sin and hate, welcoming to all who are lonely and left out, persecuted and preyed upon, who have been silenced. May we each find the grace in the way of Christ until each and every last one of us become PhD's in God's academy of love.

Amen.

Notes

1. Thomas G. Long, *Hebrews: Interpretation: A Bible Commentary for Teaching and Preaching* (Louisville: John Knox Press, 1997), 69.

2. Thomas Williams, "Saint Anselm," December 21, 2015, https://plato.stanford.edu/entries/anselm/ (accessed February 11, 2020).

3. Saint Theophan the Recluse, "The Jesus Prayer," https://www.orthodoxprayer.org/Articles_files/Theophan-Jesus%20Prayer.html (accessed February 11, 2020).

4. Richard Rohr, *Immortal Diamond: The Search for our True Self* (San Francisco: Jossey-Bass, 2013), 164–65.

5. Ibid, 173.

Anchored by Hope

Hebrews 6:13-20

Independence Day Weekend
This week, we hear the bold promise of hope at the heart of Hebrews. Just as the constitution is the foundational document of the United States, providing a framework for our freedoms, God's unfailing promise and hope to us in Christ provides the framework for our faith. Being anchored to God, church, or even a religion does not weigh us down or tie us down. Rather, having an unwavering confidence in God gives us the stability and freedom we need to live with lightness, risk, joy, and hope.

Andrew: In June 1958, a bomb rocked the Bethel Baptist Church in Birmingham, Alabama, led by the Rev. Fred L. Shuttlesworth, a civil rights bright light.

Anne: In 1963, in the same city, the 16th Street Baptist Church bombing killed four Black little girls.

Andrew: As the drive to register Black voters heated up during Freedom Summer in 1964, nearly three dozen Black churches in Mississippi were bombed or burned by white supremacists.

Anne: White hatred of Black sacred space didn't end in the 1960s. In July 1993, the FBI uncovered a plot to bomb the First A.M.E. Church in Los Angeles, wipe out its congregation with machine guns, and then assassinate Rodney G. King in hopes of provoking a race war.

Andrew: More than 100 people were arrested in connection with 225 attacks at African-American churches between 1995 and 1998. Ultimately, 25 of those arrested were charged with hate crimes.

Anne: In November 2008, three white men set the Macedonia Church of God in Christ in Springfield, Massachusetts ablaze hours after Barack Obama's election as the US's first Black president.

Andrew: While it may be Independence Day weekend on the calendar, there seems to be no end to the weak-minded white supremacy that motivates a massacre at something as sacred and safe as a prayer meeting at church. In Charleston, SC on June 17, 2015, at Mother Emanuel AME, the oldest Black church in the South, a white supremacist murdered nine people. He chose to act on the 193rd anniversary of a failed slave revolt (June 17, 1822) led by the church's founder, Denmark Vesey, a free Black man and abolitionist. Within days of that failed revolt, Vesey and five others had been tried secretly and executed.[1]

This weekend, many of us white Americans have had our fill of burgers and brats and barbeque cookouts as we celebrate the Fourth of July. We'd rather not look at a hot dog or a bowl of coleslaw for a long while. But we ought to be fed up with the fact that we still aren't free from the bondage of racism. Racism isn't a nineteenth-century problem; it's a twenty-first-century problem. We can patriotically recite the Pledge of Allegiance all we want, but doing so doesn't make "One nation, under God with liberty and justice for all" any truer. Liberty for all? Freedom for all? Who are we kidding?

The facts are overwhelming: the sickness of racism is alive and well in America. Therefore, we the people of this congregation in this city are joining churches all over our country to participate in Freedom from Racism Sunday because the struggle for freedom from racism is not a thing of the past. The vicious racism in our nation is real and persistent. Recent attacks on Black churches highlight how these "sites of love have been magnets for hate,"[2] and many people are asking why.

Two weeks after the massacre at Mother Emanuel AME Church mysterious fires broke out at *six* Black churches. Half of those fires are being investigated as arsons. The *Washington Post* attempted to answer why this is happening in a column titled "Why racists target black churches":

They have always remained a symbol of hope in the darkness of American racism and a source of leadership, political and religious, in the African-American community. Though it may seem the black church has always been a part of American culture—as essential as the Fourth of July or "The Star-Spangled Banner"—it was not always so. When human beings were held in servitude and meetings among slaves were banned, founding a black church was considered an act of rebellion.[3]

How profoundly Christian, how like the early church to which the sermon of Hebrews was delivered: founding a church was an act of rebellion. The white community needs to do some rebelling of its own these days. We need to rebel against the pervasive power and sin of racism, and to stand strong supporting our Black siblings. We need to stand with the Black church that has long been a haven of hope from racism and oppression for all those in need of prayer and healing and welcome.

Anne: We like to think of our churches in this way—as safe havens and sanctuaries—because the reality is that in so many ways our churches symbolize God to us. We want our churches to represent the One we hope in—Jesus the Christ, our Comforter and Redeemer—and all that we hope for—a peaceful, just, and loving world.

However, history has taught us the brutal lesson that our churches are not safe places. They're not immune to the ills and evils of society. Our churches have, at times, been the sources of incredible evil as well as the targets. So we learn, time and time again, that our churches are not God. Nor are our churches buildings that we can lock down and lock up. Churches are communities of people who are far from perfect and prone to all of the temptations of pride and prejudice, proving time and time again that our churches are not God and neither are Christians.

The people of the Hebrews congregation understand this. Far from perfect, they are weary from persecution, burned out on church, tired of being mocked, and fed up with defending their faith. They want to be done with this whole early church movement and just run back to the Temple, back to the place they know. Who can blame them? We all love what's familiar, what feels safe. They're at the point of defeat and retreat, of giving up hope on the way of Jesus because, honestly, it seems to be getting in the way of hope, not leading them to it.

But the preacher reminds them that Jesus is their hope, not a church or a temple. Jesus anchors them to God. When people persecute the believers,

God is with them. When oppressive systems push them to their edge, God will be there. When people are beaten down and roughed up, God will be there. God will never disappoint them. God will never persecute them. God will never break God's promises to them.

Hebrews 6:19, arguably *the* key verse of the entire book, says, "We have this hope, a sure and steadfast anchor of the soul." Or, as *The Message* puts it, "We who have run for our very lives to God have every reason to grab the promised hope with both hands and never let go. It's an unbreakable spiritual lifeline, reaching past all appearances right to the very presence of God where Jesus . . . has taken up his permanent post as high priest for us . . . ." (vv. 19-20).

The preacher of Hebrews is dealing with a bunch of tired skeptics, so he now has to remind them why God's promises can be trusted in the first place. Just as he invoked the name of Moses in chapter three, the preacher names another of their faith heroes: Abraham (v. 13).

Early on their relationship, God promised Abraham that he would have many descendants (Gen 12:2; 15:5). Then the unthinkable happened. God asked Abraham to sacrifice—to kill—his son, Isaac. How could Abraham ever have descendants without Isaac? Does God not keep God's promises? Well, you know the story. Abraham, in an absurd act of faith, hiked up the mountain, prepared an altar, and raised his hand to kill his own son. But God stopped him and provided a ram to sacrifice instead, sparking Isaac's life (Gen 22:1-14). Three verses later, God reiterates the promise to Abraham with even more power and persuasion, saying, "I will indeed bless you, and I will make your offspring as numerous as the stars of heaven and as the sand that is on the seashore" (Gen 22:17).

God follows through on God's promises, even if in absurd ways that are unknowable and incomprehensible to us. Promises from people fail, but we can trust promises from God. How can we know the difference? Well, people swear oaths on the names of something or someone with more authority than them. This authority is usually God. Think of a witness in the court being asked, "Do you solemnly swear to tell the truth, the whole truth, and nothing but the truth, so help you God?"[4]

As people, we have to swear on something higher than ourselves because, when we mess up and break our promise (which we will), there will be someone of greater repute than us to settle the dispute, someone who can and will hold us accountable. Common as it was in the ancient world, the Hebrews would have understood this oath system very well. Next in the passage, the preacher contrasts human oaths with God's oath, which cannot be broken because there is no being higher than God. You can't get a stronger promise than God promising with God's own name that God will bless you!

We don't like to look to an authority higher than ourselves when we make promises, do we? We swear to our own power, our own privileges, and our own preferences because, if we're not promising anything to anyone higher than us, then we don't have to think about other people. But if we swear our ultimate allegiance to God—not to the U.S. flag, the Confederate flag, or even the rainbow flag—then we have to consider other people. Even though considering other people is not always profitable for us or preferable to us, God considers other people.

The reality bears repeating again: we who are white may proudly profess that we are indivisible and that there is justice and liberty for all, but that simply isn't true. We are not united; we are divided. When one person or race does not have justice or liberty, then none of us do.

We want to swear that atrocities like that in Charleston will not happen again, that we will not let it happen again. But, sad as it is, as long as we are swearing on our government or looking to other people to unravel the systems ingrained in our culture and hearts, then this kind of horrific racism will continue.

The oath we must swear by, the oath that the preacher insists the Hebrew people swear by, is the promise that they will cling to Jesus with their very lives and allow him to anchor them to God. To cling to Jesus is not to sit back and watch and wait for other people to figure things out. This is our stuff to figure out. We must live like Jesus, think like Jesus, love like Jesus, see like Jesus, forgive like Jesus. We must love our neighbor just as much, or more, than we love ourselves (Mk 12:30-31). We must bring about the kingdom—the kin-dom—of God for all God's children.

Andrew: What will it take to pledge our allegiance finally and fully to bringing about the kin-dom of God for *all* children of God? It may indeed take some swearing in—and some swearing. If you think about an anchor being a hook—something that stabilizes us and keeps us from drifting—we can't let ourselves off the hook from the things that matter most to Jesus. When we let ourselves off the hook or off the anchor, what happens? Well, we drift. And we drift further and further away from Jesus' vision of the kin-dom of God.

I'm thinking of a person today who wouldn't let anyone off the hook when it came to religious freedom and human dignity, a Baptist prophet and professor and friend: James Dunn. James became a hero to a whole lot of Baptists committed to soul liberty and a proper understanding of the separation of church and state.

Did you know religious liberty has been called Baptists' greatest contribution to American culture? James knew what many of us historic Baptists know, that religious freedom and human dignity are as inseparable from American culture as parades and patriotic songs and pyrotechnics on the Fourth of July. James, who described himself as a "Texas-bred, Spirit-led, Bible-teaching, revival-preaching, recovering Southern Baptist," described human dignity as, "the spark of the Divine in all of us that prompts awe and adoration."[5] He said human dignity "is the flame worth guarding and defending in every person."[6]

This bona fide belief in the human dignity of every person is at the heart of the Black Lives Matter movement, which Alicia Garza, Patrisse Cullors, and Opal Tometi began in 2013 when George Zimmerman was acquitted in the shooting of African-American teenager Trayvon Martin.[7] Black lives matter. They don't matter to the exclusion of white lives or public servants' lives, as some critics have claimed. Rather, "Black lives matter" is a reminder and affirmation that Black people's lives are not dispensable, though Black bodies have been repeatedly brutalized and Black lives destroyed by racist institutions and individuals. Remember our Constitution, which says, "We hold these truths to be self-evident, that all men are created equal, that they are endowed by their Creator with certain unalienable Rights, that among these are Life, Liberty and the pursuit of Happiness."

Over 240 years and counting, and more than a half century after the end of the Jim Crow era, we are still struggling to find freedom at last for all of God's children.

To be anchored in hope is to be anchored in this kind of dream that twentieth-century African-American poet and social activist Langston Hughes openly shares in his poem, "Let America be America again." If only we could feel the weight of these words, and to not only be hooked on the dream of it, but to hook in to a plan of action that can help make Langston's dream our own. Letting ourselves off the hook is *not* an option. As Rev. Lee Tredwell, a beautiful queer Black man, read so passionately in today's service :

> Let America be America again.
> Let it be the dream it used to be.
> Let it be the pioneer on the plain

Seeking a home where he himself is free.
The poorest worker bartered through the years.[8]

No, when it comes to what sets *all* people free, now is no time to let ourselves off the hook. Now more than ever is the time for us to hook into the holy—to hook into the holy with the boldness and the courage shown by the families of the Charleston shooting victims when they delivered a powerful message of forgiveness to the white supremacist who murdered the people they loved the most. Such words of forgiveness: "I forgive you and have mercy on your soul. You hurt me. You hurt a lot of people, but I forgive you. We have no room for hate. We have to forgive."[9]

If there is anything that can help us believe that God's dreams for our world can come true, it's this. As my friend and mentor Bill Leonard wrote, "For some Christians the grace of forgiveness comes quickly; for others, forgiveness is a 'kingdom of God' grace that is a long time coming. Both responses are complex; both are gospel."[10] And sooner or later, it's such a grace that steadies us—the more and more that we are hooked into the holy.

Anne: What does it feel like to be "hooked into the holy?" The image of being hooked to something—like a trout hooked on a fishing line—is perhaps threatening, confining, and even painful. You know, many people feel this way about church, that it forces them into a box they don't want to be in rather than freeing them for a life they were created to thrive in.

What if being "hooked into the holy" didn't mean being weighed down by God or by church? What if we thought of being hooked into the holy in the same manner we think of being hooked into a mountain climbing harness? A harness gives you enough security to freely explore and climb the mountain before you.

Granted, some people climb mountains without a harness, but to do so requires an immense amount of skill and practice. While I myself have never climbed without being anchored, I imagine people who free climb are extremely cautious with their movements for fear of making a misstep and falling.

When your harness and climbing ropes are anchored into secure bolts in the rock above you and when you have a belayer, or anchor person, below you to catch you when you fall, then you have so much more freedom to succeed. Even when you fail, you can't fall. If you miss a hand grip or foot hold, no big deal. You just try something different next time. It's counterintuitive, but the more anchor points you have, the more risks you can take and the more freedom of mind and movement you have as you traverse the face of the rock.

This is the kind of experience that the preacher of Hebrews wants to impart to his people: being anchored to God in Jesus is not something that slows them down or weighs them down. Rather, being anchored to God gives them the security and rootedness they need to be freer in their faith. It actually lightens them.

We have witnessed such freedom and lightness with the forgiveness that Andrew has already spoken of in the people of the Emanuel AME Church in Charleston. What allows them to have faith enough to forgive their loved ones' murderer so fast and so freely? Hope. Hope in God. Not hope in humanity. Hope in God. Fred Craddock says,

> Hope . . . is presented not so much as our posture toward God and the future as it is a quality of the Christian message, real and certain in itself, however we may happen to feel on any given day. Hope is out in front of the [Hebrews], beckoning them. Hope is an anchor firm and secure in the very place where God is . . . . On occasions when we feel no hope, hope still exists . . . the Christian life is not held hostage to feelings.[11]

And my siblings in the Spirit, we must cling to this hope that breaks the captivity of the gospel in our country, a captivity that says that liberty and justice and equality and freedom are not for all, but only for some. Hope lightens us up so that we are free to continue to build the kin-dom of God instead of getting stopped in our tracks by failure or fear that what we do or say will be wrong or that it won't make a difference.

Just as a mountain climber that chooses a hand grip or foot hold that doesn't work simply tries a different one until she finds one that works and gets her one step closer to that "higher ground,"[12] we must not be afraid to try things even when we do not know if they will work, perhaps especially when we don't know if they'll work and perhaps especially when we wonder if they will make any difference at all. Because whatever we're doing right now clearly isn't working. Our country, our community, our church, must find new ways. We cannot be silent. We must take risks. And we must trust that God is our ultimate belayer, anchoring us in hope all along the way.

Our hope in God allows us to believe that despite all the odds and despite what we may be thinking in our hearts, our country is not hopeless.

We have made progress. We have come quite a ways. We cannot lose hope now. Even though we've fallen and faltered, making numerous missteps, we have to swing back on the mountain, find new foot holds, and work harder to climb even higher. With God as our belayer, our anchor of hope, we will make progress.

We must be anchored not just in the hope we have in God, but in the vision of God's kin-dom given to us by Jesus—a kin-dom like the dreamed one Langston Hughes describes. There, justice and liberty are available for all, freedom reigns supreme, and hope leads us again and again to higher ground.

Amen.

Notes

1. Michel Eric Dyson, "Love and Terror in the Black Church," *New York Times*, June 20, 2015 (accessed July 2, 2015).

2. Ibid.

3. Sarah Kaplan and Justin Wm. Moyer, "Why Racists Target Black Churches," *The Washington Post*, June 20, 2015, https://www.washingtonpost.com/news/morning-mix/wp/2015/07/01/why-racists-burn-black-churches/?tid=sm_fb (accessed July 1, 2015).

4. Fred B. Craddock, "The Letter to the Hebrews: Introduction, Commentary, and Reflections," *The New Interpreter's Bible*, XII (Nashville, TN: Abingdon Press, 1998), 80.

5. Brent Walker, "James Dunn: Champion for Religious Liberty," Smyth & Helwys Publishing (Macon, GA: 1999), 74.

6. Ibid.

7. "Herstory," *Black Lives Matter*, https://blacklivesmatter.com/about/herstory/ (accessed February 11, 2020); "Black Lives Matter," *Wikipedia*, https://en.wikipedia.org/wiki/Black_Lives_Matter (accessed February 11, 2020).

8. Langston Hughes, "Let America be American Again," *Poem Hunter*, http://www.poemhunter.com/poem/let-america-be-america-again/ (accessed July 3, 2015).

9. Inae Oh, "Families of Charleston Shooting Victims: 'We Forgive You'," *Mother Jones*, http://www.motherjones.com/mojo/2015/06/families-charleston-shooting-victims-we-forgive-you (accessed July 2, 2015).

10. Bill Leonard, "Sunday's coming: Freedom from Racism," *Baptist News Global*, http://baptistnews.com/article/sundays-coming-freedom-from-racism/#.XkLF2xNKhTY (accessed February 11, 2020).

11. Craddock, 83.

12. Reference to a hymn we sang earlier in the worship service, "Higher Ground." Lyrics by Johnson Oatman Jr. (1856-1926) and music by Charles Hutchinson Gabriel (1856-1932). "I'm pressing on the upward way / New heights I'm gaining every day; / Still praying as I onward bound, / "Lord, plant my feet on higher ground."

King Melchizedek (It's Okay, No One Else Knows who He is Either)

Hebrews 7

When someone dies, it's tempting to create a myth about who we wanted or needed them to be, rather than who they actually were. This may or may not have been the case with Melchizedek, a priest defined more by mystery than by history. We may not know a lot about him, but we know he mattered in his day. So it's probably worthwhile for us to try and figure out if his life and legacy make a difference for how we understand Jesus today.

Andrew: There is a fairly famous adage in Academy Award-winning director John Ford's 1962 western *The Man Who Shot Liberty Valance*, and it goes like this: "When the legend becomes fact, print the legend." In this film, Jimmy Stewart plays a man who becomes famous for shooting the infamous outlaw Liberty Valance. In reality, John Wayne's character shot the criminal, but he lets Stewart's character take the credit. When Jimmy Stewart tries to tell the truth to a reporter, however, he's told, "When the legend becomes fact, print the legend."[1]

Popular culture has a way of creating legends that become widely accepted truths. Stories take on a life of their own when they serve a bigger purpose, noble or not. Some people romance the story, others reconstruct it to serve their narrative. Before long, mystery defines the story more than history does, whether we're talking about Al Gore creating the internet,

The Chicago Cubs' Curse of the Billy Goat, or the version of the Old West that John Ford and John Wayne created.[2]

When someone dies, it's especially tempting to create a myth about who we wanted or needed them to be. In doing so, we lose sight of who they really were. Think of the legend of Camelot that was born out of John F. Kennedy's death and Johnny Cash's myth of the man in black. It is important to pay attention to what endures in popular imagination, because it can reveal deep truths about our motivations and the stories we want to tell and be told. This is true of popular cultural imagination and our spiritual and biblical imaginations. Today, we're introducing the myth and mystery of King Melchizedek.

Anne: While mysterious to you and me, the memory and myth of Melchizedek was fairly well known by the time of Hebrews. We've learned by now that one of the hermeneutical ploys the preacher of Hebrews uses to get his audience excited about Jesus is to show how Jesus is like their ancestral heroes of the faith, but in a more complete, fulfilled way. In chapters 3 and 6, he uses Moses and Abraham, figures the Hebrews knew well and revered highly, to give credibility to Jesus, who they didn't know as well or revere as highly. This strategy makes sense for Moses and Abraham. Their stories are well known biblical sagas that stretch over multiple chapters and entire books. But Melchizedek has no such saga, just a three-verse cameo in Genesis and a one-verse namedrop in Psalms (Gen 14:17-20; Ps 110:4).

So why does the preacher of Hebrews devote an entire chapter (plus some) to Melchizedek? He gets way more airtime than Moses and Abraham combined! Maybe it's because he's shrouded in mystery that Melchizedek makes such a great sermon illustration. You know how we preachers are with our creative, interpretive license. Because Melchizedek is a rather shadowy and elusive figure in the biblical narrative, he's ripe for myth and meaning-making. In fact, Melchizedek is mentioned in quite a few writings outside the Bible from the first five centuries AD. Not surprisingly, his encounter with Abram recorded in Genesis 14 is remembered in a myriad of ways with multiple meanings.

The Jewish philosopher Philo of Alexandria interprets the exchange of goods between Abram and Melchizedek as an act of friendship between two equals who are sharing the spoils of victory together. To me, that's like a major league coach and player sharing a pitcher of beer together after a playoff win. The rationale was, if Abram won a war, then God helped him win. That was just the theology of the day. And, since Melchizedek is a priest representing God to the people, it was just as much his victory as Abram's.[3] Other early rabbinic texts diminished Melchizedek's priesthood altogether, saying he committed a profound error by blessing Abram before blessing God. The fact he didn't have offspring proves that God punished him for his misstep. With this interpretation, to be "a priest according to the order of Melchizedek" (v. 17) is *not* a compliment.[4]

Hebrews stands within a broad interpretative tradition when it comes to Melchizedek, and many of the claims made in Hebrews would not have been accepted outside of the early Christian sphere of thinking. However, Hebrews is among the earliest sources of speculation about Melchizedek,[5] so you could say that this preacher has first dibs. And, as we'll see, he makes meaning out of the mystery of Melchizedek for the greater purpose of motivating his people to find meaning in Jesus.

Andrew: Even with all of the faithful fascination with this cagey character, the truth is that Christians would probably pay very little attention to Melchizedek if it were not for Hebrews 5–7. As far as the New Testament goes, the name Melchizedek shows up eight times, all in the book of Hebrews. But in the Old Testament, he first shows up way back in Genesis 14 where we learn that he is a priest of God Most High and King of Salem (Shalom) or king of peace.

It would help to have some background about what was going on before Abram met Melchizedek in Genesis 14. Several chapters earlier, God told Abram (who would become Abraham) to pack up his family and all his possessions, leave the only home that he'd ever known, to go to a brand new place. For all his trouble, God promised that Abram would be blessed and become the "father of many nations" (Gen 12:1-3).

Abram was still childless in Genesis 14, and he was fighting a war with all kinds of drama and strife. Abram was at a real low point of his life. On top of Abram's move and disappointed hopes and a war, a lot was going on with Lot. Lot, his family, and their possessions had been taken in a raid on Sodom by a bunch of kings. Abram took 318 of his closest friends (aka military allies) and went to rescue him. After this successful military campaign, with Lot and all his family in tow, Melchizedek unexpectedly shows up to welcome Abraham back and shine out God's glory:

> And King Melchizedek of Salem brought out bread and wine; he was priest of God Most High. He blessed him and said, "Blessed be Abram

by God Most High, maker of heaven and earth; and blessed be God Most High, who has delivered your enemies into your hand!" And Abram gave him one-tenth of everything." (Gen 14:18-20)

Here in Genesis, Melchizedek is a priest to the patriarch and a faith figure to the father of nations. Abram is a weary warrior, and Melchizedek meets him, not to glorify his military might but to *bless* him. Melchizedek, the King of Righteousness and the King of Peace, is also the High Priest of the God of gods, and he blesses Abram and seals the blessing with a basket of bread and a bottle of wine. Say, does this sound like someone else we know?

Anne: "Every time you eat this bread and drink this cup, do so in remembrance of me" (cf 1 Cor 11:26a, 24). Jesus gave us the gift of experiencing his blessing over and over again by instructing us to remember him at the Table with bread and wine. At the Table, we're not just remembering Jesus' titles or name. We're giving thanks for his inner qualities, which are lasting gifts to us: peace, justice, equality, righteousness, forgiveness, authenticity, generosity, love.

In the same way, the preacher of Hebrews brings up Melchizedek not to focus on his kingly name or priestly position, but to highlight his inner qualities, "righteousness, peace, and timelessness [which] point forward to the nature of Jesus, the true and perpetual great high priest. Theologically, the Preacher wants to say that Melchizedek is a signpost planted in the old [priestly] order indicating [that] the good gifts given to humanity in Jesus were there in God's mind from the very beginning."[6]

These good gifts from God, these inner qualities that we see in Melchizedek and then in Jesus, are what matter most. They are what differentiate the new priestly order from the former priestly one. In his opening meditations at the beginning of class, one of my favorite yoga instructors, Billy Potocnik, often says:

> Who cares if you can do a handstand if you're not a nice person? If you have washboard abs, but you don't smile at people—how are you making the world a better place? Yoga is hard. You're going to get the physical workout; I guarantee it. It's the inner transformation of your heart that needs the real work. People might look at you for a few seconds if you are super fit and muscular, but they will only be truly drawn to you in a more lasting way if you are shining your inner light,

leading from your heart, showing kindness to the world. That's what this practice is about.[7]

Another way to say this is that it's not what's on the outside but what's on the inside that counts. And this is what inspires the preacher to use Melchizedek as another way of introducing Jesus to his people. Melchizedek, and then Jesus, had inner qualities that connected them to God in ways that the former priests did not. Despite their efforts, the members of the Levitical priesthood, the old system, were ultimately not effective in helping people connect to God and attain perfection or salvation (or completeness and wholeness). Another kind of priest was needed. Jesus, like the priest-king Melchizedek who wasn't from the right bloodline but who blessed Abram anyway, is different for a few reasons:

1. Melchizedek is named in the text without reference to his mother or father. Therefore because he has no "beginning days" (birth), it's assumed he has no "ending days" (death), meaning he'll remains a priest forever (v. 3). In the old system, priests were from a certain family line and no one lasted forever because, of course, they would die. Jesus, like Melchizedek, holds his priesthood permanently; he was in the beginning with God and continues to reign forever with God. For this preacher, Jesus' divine genealogy trumps his human one.[8]
2. Just as Melchizedek blessed Abram, symbolizing the "superior blessing the inferior" (v. 7), Jesus, superior because he's without sin (v. 27), blesses all of us with a "once and for all sacrifice" even though we continue to sin. In the old system, priests had to offer sacrifices over and over again because they themselves sinned and thus their sacrifices were only temporary, not timeless.[9]
3. In the old system, priests took their office without divine oath, but Jesus became high priest with God's oath, and God's word is the first and last, as we hear in Psalm 110:4: "The Lord has sworn and will not change his mind, you are a priest forever, according to the order of Melchizedek."[10]

Understanding all of this is important because having a new priest means having a new way of doing things. God is doing something brand new in Jesus. As special as he is, even Melchizedek can't offer the grace and hope that Jesus does. Verse 12 emphasizes this distinction, saying, "For when there is a change in the priesthood, there is necessarily a change in the law as well." It's like getting a new pastor. Inevitably, some things will change when a new pastor is called to a church. They will have different ideas, different ways of doing things, different strengths and weaknesses, and a different personality and pastoral style. Getting a new priest was like that, but even greater. This change was like getting an entirely new priesthood. (By the way, the term "priest" is found 750 times in the Septuagint, the Greek translation of the Old Testament. The term "priesthood" is used only 9 times, and the only time it's used in the New Testament is in Hebrews 7:11, 12, 24).[11]

The preacher is saying to his people, "Remember how Melchizedek brought a new and different kind of blessing to your ancestors? That is what Jesus has done for you. With this new high priest, 'perfection [or wholeness] is a matter of [inner] transformation rather than [external] transaction.'[12] Jesus summed up the law in a new way with two commandments: love God and love others. It's not about living under a strict law; it's about living with a sacrificial love. Look, I know you've been operating under the Levitical priesthood your whole lives and you expect God to continue working in this system, but God is doing a new thing. Jesus is your great high priest now. And he's doing things differently."

Looking to Jesus as "high priest" was such a radical notion, given how ingrained they were in the Levitical priesthood system. It's no wonder they were struggling to wrap their minds around Jesus. It would be like someone telling us that when something is broken in our country, we're not going to fix it by using the three-branch government system that we have, like by voting in a different president, or passing a new bill. Instead, we're going to bring in a King or Queen and go with a monarchy. What would you think about that?

It's not a perfect analogy, but do you see how radical a change accepting Jesus as "high priest" was for the Hebrew people? However, because Melchizedek was outside of the priesthood their ancestors were used to, the preacher is hoping that they see the parallel and that they will accept Jesus just as their ancestors accepted Melchizedek.

He's also hoping that they'll see that the priesthood of Jesus is simply trying to get back to the original intention of the old priesthood—to be in a covenant relationship with God. Jesus said, "Do not think that I have come to abolish the law or the prophets; I have come not to abolish but to fulfill" (Matt 5:17). The old priesthood wasn't wrong; it was just incomplete. Scholar Tom Wright points out that:

The word 'better' [in the Greek] occurs more times in Hebrews than in the whole rest of the New Testament put together. That tells us something about the way the writer thinks. He is constantly contrasting, not something bad with something good, but something good with something better. He is not saying that the ancient Israelite system was a bad thing, with its Temple, its law and its Levitical priesthood. What he is saying is that the new dispensation which has arrived in and through Jesus is even better than what went before . . . [13]

Andrew: One of my favorite authors, Anne Lamott, once posted on her Facebook page that at 32 years old, she woke up "drunk as a skunk" most days with the added cocktail of shame and sickness and confusion to go along with it.[14] She says that in recovery, they "never EVER give up on anyone, no matter what it looks like, no matter how long it takes. Grace bats last."[15] Baseball enthusiasts would say that "grace bats cleanup." Someone batting cleanup is the strongest hitter in the lineup and bats fourth, when the first three batters are hopefully already on base.

This is what Hebrews is saying about Jesus being "a priest forever, according to the order of Melchizedek" (7:17). In other words, Jesus is God's cleanup batter, which means that grace is the sweet spot in God's lineup of patriarchs and prophets and priests and kings. From Lot to Anne Lamott, from Melchizedek to the Messiah, from Genesis to Jesus, God is alive and at work transforming something good into something even better, saving the best till last, and changing the water of the old order of things into the wine of the new order of things. We're not talking about the wine of the world that Anne Lamott talks about, but rather the wine of the Word made flesh. Not a wine that makes you want more once you get to the bottom of the bottle because it is never enough, but a wine that satisfies fully and finally. There is no bottom to this kind of wine. It is the wine of God's grace.

And once you have tasted of the wine of the Word made flesh, we find out that there is a grace that never runs out, a grace that fills us with life that really is life. Or in the words of preacher and professor Tom Long:

> Like the wedding miracle at Cana, Jesus is God's very best wine, saved for the last but ready from the dawn of creation. There were foretastes of this magnificent vintage, indeed—most remarkably in this impressive and elusive figure Melchizedek, who was an anticipatory sip poured into

the glass of the old order. Melchizedek was the bouquet of the wine yet to come."[16]

The mythology of Melchizedek finally gives clarity and character and a foretaste of the joy of God in Jesus. It is the full-bodied revelation of God in the person of Jesus. To mix my metaphors, Jesus is God's best wine that never runs out. Jesus is the human face of God's grace; a grace that bats last and is the final word on things. Christ who comes like Melchizedek did to Abraham in order to bless weary warriors like us, to give the wine of joy to the tired and brokenhearted like us, to offer the bread of heaven to the wounded and troubled like us. And it is precisely this completeness and fullness in Christ that reveals God's legendary character of love—a love that is larger than life, a love that reveals the Jesus of history and the Christ of mystery—and reveals the God of grace that makes this all so holy and all so human.

Amen.

Notes

1. Oreo, "When the legend becomes fact . . . print the legend," *Daily Kos*, Sept 7, 2006, http://www.dailykos.com/story/2006/09/07/243676/-When-the-legend-becomes-fact-print-the-legend# (accessed July 10, 2015).

2. Roger Ebert, "The Man Who Shot Liberty Valance," *RogerEbert.com*, Dec 28, 2011, http://www.rogerebert.com/reviews/great-movie-the-man-who-shot-liberty-valance-1962 (accessed July 10, 2015).

3. Luke Timothy Johnson, *Hebrews: A Commentary*, (Louisville, KY: Westminster John Knox Press, 2006), 182.

4. Johnson, *Hebrews*, 183.

5. Johnson, *Hebrews*, 181.

6. Thomas G. Long, "Hebrews," *Interpretation: A Bible Commentary for Teaching and Preaching* (Louisville, KY: Westminster John Knox Press, 1997), 85.

7. Paraphrased from Billy Potocnik's opening meditations in his yoga classes at *Pura Vida Fitness and Spa* in Denver, CO (2015).

8. Long, *Hebrews*, 84-85.

9. Long, *Hebrews*, 86.

10. Long, *Hebrews*, 88.

11. Johnson, *Hebrews*, 185.

12. Ibid.

13. Tom Wright, *Hebrews for Everyone* (Louisville, KY: Westminster John Knox Press, 2003), 76.

14. Anne Lamott, in an untitled blog entry on her Facebook page from July 7, 2015 (accessed July 9, 2015), https://www.facebook.com/AnneLamott/posts/699854196810893?fref=nf&pnref=story.

15. Ibid.

16. Thomas G. Long, "Hebrews," *Interpretation: A Bible Commentary for Teaching and Preaching* (Louisville, KY: Westminster John Knox Press, 1997), 85.

9

Jesus: The People's Priest

Hebrews 8

The author of Hebrews praises Jesus as the high priest. Just as people today are drawn to Pope Francis because he genuinely seems to care about people more than power, we are drawn to Jesus because of his compassion, not his position. The persuasion of Jesus' power comes not from his biblical position as high priest, but from the presence of God within him that he shared so freely with those around him. In a culture that defines who we are by what we do, Jesus empowers us to define who we are by how we are: how we love, how we serve, how we forgive, and how we relate to God and the world.

Anne: After flittering and flying around the meandering 28 verses of chapter 7 last week, all about the myth and mystery of Melchizedek, today we land gently and swiftly on a very short and sweet chapter 8. Verse one starts off, "Now the main point in what we are saying is this . . . " (8:1).

So, no big deal if you missed last week. Melchizedek Shmelzedek! Today we get back to the main point of it all—Jesus. Now, I can hear some of you who were here last week thinking to yourself, "You mean I didn't have to be here? I could have been in the mountains or meeting friends for brunch or sitting at Starbucks with my coffee and crossword?" Well, yes, but the fact that you've done the hard work and slogged through chapter 7 means chapter 8 will be all the more richer and meaningful for you. It's like the difference between actually reading Harper Lee's much-talked about novel, *Go Set a Watchmen*, versus reading everyone else's thoughts and opinions about it. Whether or not you liked the Melchizedek chapter is beside the point. You've read it and are all the wiser because of it. Hebrews 8 will have texture and nuance for you that it wouldn't have if you didn't read chapter 7.

Regardless, we are *all* are together here in verse 1: "Now the main point in what we are saying is this." Midway through a long sermon, the preacher is giving his people a verbal cue to sit up and pay attention. Snap out of your drifting daydreams and focus in again on the word at hand. And what is the main point? Well, the preacher has several points. Go figure! Let's follow them verse-by-verse:

- Verse 1: We have a high priest whose authority is on par with God's authority. (It's divine, not human.)
- Verse 2: This priest "conducts worship in the one true sanctuary built by God" (8:2, *The Message*). (In other words, the sanctuary is in heaven, not here on earth)
- Verses 3-5: This priest offers sacrifices like all the others, but there's still something different about him. He worships in the heavenly sanctuary of God, forever in God's presence—not in the makeshift model on earth created by man, where, like Moses, you only catch a glimpse of God. For the philosophers in the room, the words, "they offer worship in a sanctuary that is a sketch and shadow of the heavenly one" (v. 5) is most likely a reference to Philo of Alexandria, a philosopher who reinterpreted Judaism for the cultured and philosophical minds of Hellenized Alexandria, who utilized Plato's understanding that "the REAL consisted of invisible forms and ideas of which the earthly and material is but a shadow."[1] In other words, the worship tent or tabernacle on earth is a mere shadow of the real thing in heaven; it's not the thing itself.[2]
- Verses 6-7: But Jesus (ah, there it is, this high priest's name) has a more excellent ministry because he doesn't just have a better covenant than the others, he *is* the better covenant, the best mediator of all between people and God.
- Verses 8-12: Why do we know that Jesus, this great high priest, is the better covenant? Because the Bible tells us so. These five verses are a direct quote from Jeremiah 31:31-34, and they're all about God making a new covenant because the people didn't keep the old one correctly.

- And Verse 13: Jesus, this new high priest, this new covenant, is replacing the old covenant, the old system. He's the real deal in a whole new way. Out with the old, in with the new.

To use an example, let's just say for the sake of argument that we believe electric cars are God's new covenant with us, and gasoline cars are the old covenant. So it's as if the preacher of Hebrews is saying that Jesus is not a replacement part for the ever-reliable and popular Toyota Camry. Jesus is a whole new kind of driving experience altogether. Let's say an electric Model S Tesla.

Yes, just like the Levitical law has been the norm forever, Camry's have been voted the "best-selling car in America for the past 12 years straight,"[3] but (and I quote this from Tesla's website):

> Unlike a gasoline internal combustion engine with hundreds of moving parts, Tesla electric motors have only one moving piece: the rotor. As a result, Model S acceleration is instantaneous, silent and smooth. Step on the accelerator and in as little as 2.8 seconds Model S is travelling 60 miles per hour, without hesitation, and without a drop of gasoline. Model S is an evolution in automobile engineering.[4]

Well, well, well. Pretty impressive right?

So, is there anything wrong with the Toyota Camry? No. But if your goal is a different driving experience all together, then an updated part on the regular old Camry isn't going to cut it. Yet just as we couldn't have discovered the technology for the electric car without discovering and refining the gasoline-fueled car first, Jesus can't be the "new covenant" without the existence of the "old covenant." One builds on the other.

That's the point of Hebrews 8 in a nutshell. We have this new covenant in Jesus, and it's different than the old one, and Jeremiah (of all people) tells us how it's different. Note that this is not a New Testament text saying that Jesus (the new covenant) is better than Israel (the old covenant). This is someone within the original Hebrew Bible context, a prophet of the people of the old covenant, saying that a new covenant is coming. Of course, Jeremiah doesn't name Jesus, but there is a clear sense from within the old covenant system that change—however it will come—is desperately needed.

Interestingly, Hebrews's use of Jeremiah 31:31-34 is the lengthiest quotation of Old Testament text in the entire New Testament. The original passage comes from the series of prophesies in Jeremiah 30–33 offering hope to the Israelites who are in exile, hope of being of restored to their homeland. However, "the return to [their homeland] will not mean simply a return to the covenant made at Sinai; there will be a new covenant relationship between God and Israel that will be qualitatively different."[5] In Jeremiah, "the new covenant promises the inscribing of God's law on the hearts of believers and the forgiveness of sins."[6] It isn't so much an new content, but a new manner way that content (the law) is presented.

I love the way Eugene Peterson describes this new covenant in his paraphrase of Hebrews 8:8-12 (*The Message*):

> This new plan I'm making with Israel isn't going to be written on paper, isn't going to be chiseled in stone. This time I'm writing out the plan in them, carving it on the lining of their hearts. I'll be their God, they'll be my people. They won't go to school to learn about me, or buy a book called *God in Five Easy Lessons*. They'll all get to know me firsthand, the little and the big, the small and the great. They'll get to know me by being kindly forgiven, with the slate of their sins forever wiped clean.

You can't buy a book called *God in Five Easy Lessons* and know what there is to know about God's heart, God's character, or the depth of God's love for us. If you could, you wouldn't be here today, and I wouldn't either. I'd have five sermons and then be out of a job! The author of Jeremiah says you can only get at this knowledge of God through the heart. And the author of Hebrews says the way God gets at our hearts to "imprint" (1:3) them with this love is through Jesus, our great high priest. Notice that verse 6 says, "Jesus has obtained a more excellent ministry." What is ministry but incarnational interaction, face-to-face relationships, and real life experience? If God is our God, and we are God's people, how do we, the people "from the least to the greatest" (v. 11), come to know God? It's through Jesus—through his life and ministry and mostly through the fact that he forgives our sins. His inner nature is forgiveness. You can't get forgiveness in a book. You can only get it in person. Remember these scenes?

- Jesus calling Zacchaeus, the tax collector, down from the tree and telling him he'd like to be a guest in his home (Luke 19)

- Jesus asking for water from the Samaritan woman at the well, releasing her from the burden of the judgment in which she lives and giving her living water so she will never thirst again (John 4)
- Jesus saying to those ridiculing and lifting stones to throw at the woman caught in adultery, "Let anyone among you who is without sin be the first to cast a stone" (John 8:7), then blessing her before she went on her way
- Jesus saying on behalf of his crucifiers, "Father forgive them for they know not what they are doing" (Luke 23:34), even as they were killing him and casting lots for his clothing

This not the kind of forgiveness you read about in a "how-to" manual. You can only experience it through encounters of real and radical love.

Reading about experiences don't always teach us how to fully accomplish or replicate them. For example, Damon and I got a new puppy on Wednesday night, an 8-week-old golden retriever named Deacon. We've been talking about getting a puppy since we first met over 3 years ago. We spent at least 3 months really looking for a puppy and figuring out the best time to get him, and we spent the past 3 weeks asking people about their puppy raising tips, watching Zak George's Dog Training rEvolution videos on YouTube, and reading books like *The Puppy Primer, How to Behave So Your Dog Behaves*, and *The Perfect Puppy: How to Raise a Well-Behaved Dog*.

Three years, three months, and three weeks later, we've now had our puppy for three days. And let me tell you, reading the books and watching the videos are one thing; actually trying to raise a puppy is another. Deacon is adorable, but he's more "devilish" than "deacon" right now! We're so excited to have him, but training him will take hard work and a lot of one-on-one time with him. You can't just read the books; you have to spend the time investing in him. We knew this of course. It's like any "how-to" book in life. It helps to have the book knowledge, the written word, but until you actually train the puppy or cook that Thanksgiving turkey or knock down a wall in your house or change the oil in your car, "how-to" videos will only get you so far. The real-life experience makes the difference, and it's even better when you can have a real, live teacher there to show you in person.

That's what Jesus is. He's our real, live person showing us what love and forgiveness look like. They were written down in the law, in the first covenant, for years. But it's not until we received this second covenant—the person and ministry of Jesus—that we began to understand just what God meant by his love and grace and forgiveness. We look at Jesus' life and we can see it; we come to the Lord's Table for communion and we can experience it, and as we serve others, we can live it.

One of the best "Jesus" examples out there right now is Pope Francis. In 2013, *TIME* Magazine named Pope Francis the Person of the Year, calling him "the People's Pope." Aren't all Popes meant to serve and minister to the people? Yes, of course. But some popes have seemed to be more comfortable serving as figureheads than serving on the front lines with the people. Pope Francis is different. *TIME* writes:

> . . . what makes this Pope so important is the speed with which he has captured the imaginations of millions who had given up on hoping for the church at all . . . In a matter of months, Francis has elevated the healing mission of the church—the church as servant and comforter of hurting people in an often harsh world—above [the doctrinal work of his predecessors].[7]

Few people are compelled by doctrine. Most people are compelled by love that is lived out in front of them. The Pope says:

> Argue less, accomplish more . . . We have a glut of problems to tackle. Stop bickering and roll up your sleeves. Don't let the perfect be the enemy of the good . . . I prefer a Church which is bruised, hurting and dirty because it has been out on the streets, rather than a Church which is unhealthy from being confined and from clinging to its own security."[8]

Pope Francis has made it clear that he does not just want talk, but transformation. He has indeed demonstrated his kindness and compassion for the poor and the marginalized:

- He visited the Philippines in January 2015 to meet the victims of typhoon Yolanda.
- He washed the feet of a Muslim woman jailed in Rome's youth prison as part of the Holy Thursday ceremony. (This was the first time the ceremony was taken to a youth prison and the first time women were included in the ritual.)

- He touched, kissed, and blessed a man covered in tumors after the general audience held in St. Peter's square in Vatican in a manner akin to the story of Jesus healing and touching lepers.
- He celebrated his 77th birthday with three homeless people, sharing his birthday breakfast with them and treating them like family.
- He makes himself more accessible to the people, allowing children to come near him in public appearances.
- He continues to live a modest life, preferring to stay in ordinary hotels, ride in ordinary cars, and wear plain white robes with the expensive traditional red shoes.
- He cares more about people than profits, lamenting what he calls "savage capitalism." He's asked, "How can it be that it is not a news item when an elderly homeless person dies of exposure, but it is news when the stock market loses two points?"
- He's taken a more progressive approach toward non-believers and members of the LGBTQ community, saying, "God's mercy is limitless . . . If someone is gay and is looking for the Lord, who am I to judge him?"[9]
- He's taken a strong stance on climate change, wanting us to exercise radical, beneficial stewardship to save our planet.[10]

Pope Francis has put a positive face on Catholicism for many people who did not see or experience such positivity before. He's the People's Pope because he prefers to live like the people and spend time with the people. He cares about people. He's relational.

These same characteristics and actions make Jesus "the people's priest." All priests, including those in the old Levitical system, were mediators of God's covenant, connecting the people to God and vice versa. But what was that connection about? It was about continual sacrifice to appease God because people never felt they were measuring up. They were always sinning, so they always needed forgiving.

Well, not much has changed there for us. But what has changed is the fact that Jesus, the great high priest, has come. According to Hebrews, he forgives all our sins in one fell swoop, and then gets busy helping us learn how to live "the abundant life" as he says in John 10:10. You won't find Jesus lingering around sin long in the gospels. Jesus looks at what is separating someone from God in their life (adultery, dishonesty, greed, etc.), names it directly, forgives it unconditionally, and then spends the majority of his time with the person helping them figure out where to go from here, how to live an abundant life. He doesn't make them grovel for hours to get forgiveness. It's the first thing he gives them—and often, it's his first word.

Story after story in the gospels is about Jesus being with the people, trying to help them live as the best possible versions of themselves. Jesus is the people's priest because of his compassion for people but also for his passion for progress—moving forward and living life abundantly with God. We're not stuck in our past, not lost in our future, but fully alive, here and now, in our present. In a culture that defines who we are by what we do, Jesus empowers us to define ourselves by how we are: how we love, how we serve, how we forgive, and how we relate to God and the world.

Jesus is a priest who cares less about positional authority (his office in the priesthood) and a whole lot more about personal authority (living out the call God has given him to be Incarnate Love on earth). His persuasion is based on the character of his person. It's not about his position or prestige. It's about the presence of God living in him and seen through him by his words and deeds.

And Jesus is a priest for the people because he gives us a purpose. He helps us know what to do with our lives. When you look closely at the accounts of his ministry in the Gospels, they really are less about who Jesus is an much more about what he offers. What he offers is himself: his time, his love, his forgiveness, and his guidance. He gives us himself. He spends the time it takes to actually write a law on our hearts. It's easy and takes no time or personal investment to hand someone a book of things to do. It takes a lot of time and a lot of personal investment to really teach someone about life and living, so much so that those lessons live on in their heart. When someone dies, we talk about this a lot—how their lessons and love and legacy live on in our own hearts and lives. But what if we began talking about such things earlier in life? Say, with our kids?

We ask our children, "*What* do you want to be when you grow up?" What if we asked them, "*How* do you want to be when you grow up?" Said another way, "What do you want to be *like* when you grow up?" For example, if we ask our son what he wants to be when he grows up, he might say "a firefighter." That is great. What if we followed up by asking him about the characteristics that makes a good firefighter, asking "How do you want to be a firefighter when you grow up?" The answer might be "courageous, brave, disciplined, servant-hearted, kind, strong, etc." These things describe a firefighter, but they don't limit you only to firefighting. They are lasting character traits that, if developed, will serve the child well in any field or practice he chooses.

Our kids change their minds about what they want to be when they grow up about a bazillion times. I wanted to be an astronaut, a teacher, a librarian, a pediatric orthopedic surgeon, a grocery store clerk, a math teacher, a writer, and a biologist, just to name a few. If we ask our kids "how" they want to be when they grow up, the "what" will fall into place. Whatever path they choose will be richer and deeper because they've been nurturing and developing their inner life and heart from the start.

The great thing is we're never too old to begin again when it comes to letting Christ write God's love on our hearts. We may know some things about our faith in our heads, but until we start exploring those things in our hearts, our lives won't change. And following Jesus, put simply, is changing our lives to align with the life Jesus lived: a life of experiencing and sharing God's love with all God's people.

You are included in that love. God loves you. There is nothing you have done that could make God love you less and there is nothing you can do to make God love you more. The law of the love of God is already written on your heart. It has always been there, and it's not going anywhere. But are you aware of it? Do you feel it stirring? Do you feel God's love within you? Do you feel that Jesus is your priest, that you are worthy of such love? You are. You are loved. You are forgiven. You are good enough as you are right now. And you are capable of becoming all God dreams for you to be. If a priest does anything, he reminds people of their connection to God. He tethers them to that hope that will never let them go.

Not surprisingly, the heart of Hebrews is found, in part, in a Hebrew Scripture, Jeremiah 31: "I will put my laws in their minds, and write them on their hearts, and I will be their God, and they shall be my people. And they shall not teach one another or say to each other, 'Know the Lord,' for they shall all know me, from the least of them to the greatest'"(Heb 8:10-11; Jer 31:33-34).

The heart of Hebrews is the hope of God's love living forever within us, and Jesus is at the heart of that hope. I think that's what people mean when they say, "Have you accepted Jesus into your heart?" It's not a cliché phrase, although we often make it that. It's a real question.

Does the spirit of Jesus live in your heart? Are you transformed because you know of the love and grace of Jesus? Are you transformed enough that you too can withhold judgment and serve as a priest to other people, connecting them to God by extending forgiveness and sharing love and serving their needs? We know our hearts are transformed when our lives start to serve others more than ourselves.

Jesus is our real live teacher on these things. But his teaching depends on us keeping his lessons alive with our lives. The people won't know they have a priest unless we live and serve and act as that high priest to one another. It matters who we are; we are God's people. But it matters even more how we are: living and serving as Jesus did. Because the more we do this, the more other people come to know that they are God's people too.

Yes, Jesus is the people's priest. But we are the people of Jesus, called to embody his priestly ministry to the world, called to show people that the law of God's love is inscribed so deeply in our hearts that it is seen in the living of our lives.

Amen.

Notes

1. Fred B. Craddock, "The Letter to the Hebrews: Introduction, Commentary, and Reflections" *The New Interpreter's Bible*, Volume XII (Nashville, TN: Abingdon Press, 1998), 98.

2. New Testament scholar Luke Timothy Johnson says, "[There is a kind of] Platonic worldview of Hebrews . . . [that] marries the philosophical dualism of Greek philosophy to biblical cosmology. The noun *typos* [is used here in the text] . . . within a Platonic framework, the ideal or spiritual realm holds the *typoi* of which the material representations are mere copies or imitations. The imitation depends on the ideal type, so there is a real connection, but it is always derivative and secondary." Luke Timothy Johnson, *Hebrews: A Commentary* (Louisville: Westminster John Knox Press, 2006), 201–02.

3. Bill Griffith, "Toyota's 2015 Camry: Still Sitting on Top" *Boston.com*, Dec 14, 2014, http://www.boston.com/cars/news-and-reviews/2014/12/14/toyota-camry-still-sitting-top/z1tbZbKQRodFun4okLn3ZP/story.html (accessed July 19, 2015).

4. "Models," *Tesla*, http://www.teslamotors.com/models (accessed July 19, 2015).

5. Craddock, *Hebrews*, 101.

6. Ibid

7. Howard Chua-Eoan and Elizabeth Dias, "Pope Francis, The People's Pope," *TIME*, Dec 11, 2013, http://poy.time.com/2013/12/11/person-of-the-year-pope-francis-the-peoples-pope/print/ (accessed July 18, 2015).

8. Ibid.

9. Marisse Panaligan, "Profile: Why Pope Francis Is the People's Pope," *GMA News Online*, Oct 14, 2014, http://www.gmanetwork.com/news/popefrancis/story/383550/profile-why-pope-francis-is-the-people-s-pope (accessed Feb 11, 2020).

10. Marisse Panaligan, "Profile: Why Pope Francis Is the People's Pope," *GMA News Online*, Oct 14, 2014, http://www.gmanetwork.com/news/popefrancis/story/383550/profile-why-pope-francis-is-the-people-s-pope (accessed July 18, 2015).

10

At-one-ment, Part One: A Sacrifice Worth Saving?

Hebrews 9

It's been said that "Jesus was the sacrifice to end all sacrifices."[1] In the religious practice of the day, repeated sacrifice was essential to be in right relationship with God and it was an acceptable practice of scapegoating the "other," pinning blame on someone or something else to absolve oneself of guilt or eliminate ones sins. In this context, it's easy to see how understanding Jesus' death as a "sacrifice to end all sacrifices" was good news, for it revolutionized how people saw themselves in relation to God and how they treated one another. This good news holds true for us today. It has the power to break us out of old habits of thinking and transform our understanding of the meaning of Jesus' death and the deeper meaning of all who suffer.

Anne: It's okay if you do it. Most of America does. You don't have to hide it or make excuses to justify it. I do it too: I watch reality TV.

From Robin Leach enlightening us on "The Lifestyles of the Rich and Famous" to National Geographic's documentary "Inside the White House," allowing us to tour the nooks and crannies of the nation's most highly guarded home, to ABC's "The Bachelorette" giving our hearts a chance to break as a woman sorts through 25 men to find true love, to the History Channel's survival show "Alone," taking us on a suspenseful adventure as adults try to survive by themselves in the harsh wilderness with unforgiving weather and deadly predators all around, at some point, almost all of us have become engrossed in a reality show or documentary about some reality other than our own.

Why are we obsessed with watching somebody else live their life? It's not as if we need to know this stuff for ourselves. I mean, really, how many of us will ever be rich and famous, president of the United States, date 25 people at once, or try to survive alone in the wilderness? Exactly! Yet, we use precious hours of our lives to watch other people live theirs.

I think we do this because we're curious, but there's something more to it than sheer curiosity (or boredom). I think we crave something deeper in our own lives, so much so that we look in on other people's lives to see if they have what we don't, to see if we can find what we're looking for through their lives.

This is what's happening in today's text. The people "still haven't found what they're looking for" (thank you, U2) and it's no wonder because they are not allowed to go into the very place where they would look! So what does the Preacher do? He takes his camera crew inside the Tabernacle and films his own documentary, "Inside the Holy of Holies." And all the people tune in. Wouldn't you? Unlike reality TV or documentaries about places that have nothing to do with us, the "Holy of Holies" has everything to do with us. Where God is, there we long to be too.

If you'd been excluded your whole life from the one place where you could actually meet God, wouldn't you jump at the chance to get an insider's view? Day after day, week after week, the priests burn incense on the altar within this holy place (Luke 1:8-11), and once a year in the "Holy of Holies" the real action happens: the blood of bulls and goats becomes the means of the people's repentance and God's forgiveness. Well, at least they were told this happened. They had never seen it for themselves, which is why the Preacher pulls back the curtain to reveal all.

It'd be like standing outside an arena waiting in line to get tickets to see your favorite band, but they sell out before you can get one. Then, as you are straining from the outside to hear the music inside, someone grabs you and takes you inside. Not only do you all of the sudden have a ticket to the concert, they give you a VIP pass to go backstage, hang out in the green room, and meet the band. What an experience to go from being a complete outsider to a total insider.

In today's text, the preacher gives us a backstage tour of the secret practices of the Levitical priests in the desert tabernacle. The tabernacle (*mishkan*, "residence" or "dwelling place") was the portable dwelling place for the presence of God from the time of the Exodus from Egypt to the conquering of the land of Canaan. It's described in Exodus in detail (25:1–31:11, 36:2–39:43, 40:1-38). The Hebrews version, while it follows Exodus for the most part, is slightly different.[2]

The tabernacle, or sanctuary, was a tent divided by curtains into two chambers. In the first chamber was the lamp stand (Ex 25:31-39) and the table with the bread of the Presence (Ex 25:23-30). This, says the preacher of Hebrews, is the part that's "holy" (9:2), but soon he shows them a space that is even more sacred.

Behind the second curtain is the "Holy of Holies," where only the high priest is allowed to go. It has sacred objects the people had only heard about but never seen: the golden incense altar, the Ark of the Covenant covered with gold. Inside the arc are the golden jar of manna and Aaron's rod (Ex 16:33-34, Num 17:1-11), the two tablets of the Decalogue (the Ten Commandments) from Sinai (1 Kings 9:8). On the top of the arc is the golden mercy seat with its two pure gold cherubim (Ex 25:17-21). Gold is everywhere, adorning these most holy and sacred symbols of the covenant. "Lifestyles of the Rich and Famous" indeed.

Can you imagine being told all about such beauty but never seeing it yourself? Imagine this: it's the first Sunday of the month. You walk into worship and there's a big curtain around the Communion Table. You think you can hear the pastors saying the words of institution, and maybe you can even smell the bread and juice, but you can't see a thing. The ushers are keeping you away so you can't even get in close to try to get a peek. After a while we pastors step out from the curtain and, wiping our hands, we say, "Okay, folks. You're all good. Communion is finished; your sins are forgiven. Now for our song of response."

What if Communion was like this? Can you imagine listening to a few pastors have this experience with God involving taste, sound, scent, touch, and sight, but you were excluded? They would experience this most holy of encounters with God for themselves, but also on your behalf.

This is what the people back then felt with the Levitical sacrificial system. They could faintly smell the incense being used inside the holy place, and they heard animals being slaughtered, but that's it. It wasn't their own spiritual experience. They were attempting to live vicariously through the priests. No wonder they were burned out on religion! It was all the pomp and circumstance without any of the personal and spiritual encounter. The people were shut out of the most important act in their covenant with God. They were bystanders, not participants, in their own forgiveness. How can you experience the passion of your faith without being in the presence of

God yourself? The preacher knows his people feel like outsiders in their own faith, longing to become insiders again.

Anne: There may be a secret (or not-so-secret) psychology to feeling like insiders, to believing that we have the all-access pass to information and experiences that many others don't. There are powerful feelings of reward to feeling like we belong to a group because it satisfies our hunger for social approval. There are powerful and positive feelings of being accepted by God too, of course—the power of "getting it" spiritually and being trusted with certain theological knowledge or the practical know-hows of a faith community. With this sense of exclusivity, if you think Hebrews is a complicated and hard book to understand, you're not the only one! This is not a book written for folks who are unfamiliar with the biblical world or who are first-timers to faith. The preacher of Hebrews is talking to this community using complicated images and metaphors. Frankly, he's using a good bit of "insider talk" that we might not naturally understand at first. It might even feel like we're eavesdropping on a private conversation that we can't quite sort out.

For instance, you might wonder why or how it came to be that Israelites made a sacrifice—a blood sacrifice—to please God. By extension, you may wonder why or how the belief and practice of animal sacrifice created a foundation by which the New Testament, including the writer of Hebrews, can talk about Jesus as the one who died "once for all," the final blood sacrifice that human beings will ever need to be "at one" with God and one other. Blood sacrifice is such a theological and liturgical assumption made in the Bible that it would be a natural thing for us to tap the biblical brakes for a second and ask, "Wait, what?!"

You see, in the history of Christian theology, many different theories and analogies and metaphors have been used to try and make sense of God's salvation of the world through the revelation of Jesus. The theme of sacrifice was prominent in the early church because sacrifice was so important in the worshiping life of the Hebrew people. A blood sacrifice was a perfectly acceptable way of restoring union with God. Ancients took it for granted. In the ancient world, most people lived in close contact with animals. If there were a feast to be prepared, an animal would need to be killed. It was an ordinary part of social life.

This came to apply to the divine life, too, in relationship to God. This practice was well known in the ancient world, so much so that Hebrews puts it plainly, saying, "Without shedding of blood there is no forgiveness of sins" (v. 22). This concept would not be new information to the congregation in Hebrews. In fact, in this chapter alone, all sorts of insider talk about blood has been made: "blood provides entrance before God (9:7), purification of the conscience (9:14), inauguration of a covenant (9:18), cleansing of those entering a covenant (9:19), and purifying of almost everything" (9:22).[3]

Enter into this understanding of temple sacrifice in Jerusalem, the importance of Jesus' death as a sacrificial offering. In today's text, Hebrews affirms that Jesus' blood is what creates a new covenant and the long-term benefits that come with it (see Heb 9:11-14).

With all of this bloody business of sacrifice, you might think that the enlightened writer of Hebrews would criticize the history of killing animals as the way to gain spiritual benefits. Instead, we find that Christ's sacrifice is better than all of Israel's previous practices of sacrifice because, before, the high priest would have to offer sacrifices again and again and again with blood that was not his own. But Jesus' shed blood is, ". . . a sacrifice to end sacrifice."[4]

Another theologian has helped me think about this idea more directly, too. It seems Hebrews is saying that Christ has come to put an end to blood sacrifice! The violence done to Jesus that ended his life, the horror that any of us would feel over "the cruel torture and killing of an innocent friend,"[5] is enough to make any of us biblical amateurs say, "This cannot and should not happen anymore."

Scholar Mark Heim says, "If you believe in sacrifice, then you can't practice [blood sacrifice] anymore, because it has been done completely, once and for all. This was the sacrifice to end sacrifice. Hebrews is rife with the language of liturgy and ritual, but its premise is the very opposite of what ritual [of sacrifice] presumes: not repetition but finality."[6]

While Hebrews (much to my theological chagrin) accepts the past history of sacrifice, the writer puts an entirely different spin on it that is of the utmost importance. Mark Heim, says it best: "Christ, our high priest, has offered the one needful sacrifice and makes intercession in heaven for us. No further earthly sacrifice is expected, accepted, or even possible. Jesus, on the cross, speaks the one word that otherwise can never be said of sacrifice: 'It is finished.' What sacrifice is always being repeated to achieve has actually been accomplished."[7]

Andrew: Sacrifice—the very word itself—probably conjures up a whole cadre of images and associations, noble to nebulous; spiritual to sensational, mysterious to misunderstood, idealistic to profoundly realistic.

Remember the words of Hebrews: " . . . he has appeared once for all at the end of the age to remove sin by the sacrifice of himself" (v. 26).

As ironic as it is, the whole point of Hebrews' use of the language and theological purpose of sacrifice is to say that Christ came to do away with it—not to repeat the imperfect sacrifices of the past but rather to find a way toward a vision for our lives and God's world that turns the violent aspects of sacrifice upside down. We are not to copy the cross any more than we should copy the practices of the priests in the ritual of Temple sacrifice. If indeed the sacrifice of Jesus' life was to end sacrifice altogether, then it is a sacrifice to end senseless suffering and bloodletting and scapegoating altogether.

I quote the words of Mark Heim, who has done profound theological work on this subject, once again:

> The simple idea that if we wish to follow Jesus we should aim to be crucified makes no more sense than the idea that if we should seek to be like God we should try to create a universe in six days . . . Redemptive violence is what we are to be saved from, not what we are to copy, either as perpetrators or as victims. Jesus' own saying, "If any want to become my followers, let them deny themselves and take up their cross daily and follow me" (Luke 9:23), points toward the redefinition of sacrifice we have seen in the early church. The cross of execution is an evil Jesus bears as part of a unique redemptive act. He speaks to his disciples of taking up their cross daily, uprooting it from a fixed site as an instrument of execution and making it the sign of an ongoing way of life, a "living sacrifice."[8]

There we have it: a *living* sacrifice. This is the sacrifice worth saving, but it is sacrifice of a different kind altogether. This is the sort of sacrifice that Hebrews will describe later as, "a sacrifice of praise to God, that is, the fruit of our lips that confess his name. (13:15). The passage goes on to say, "Do not neglect to do good and to share what you have, for such sacrifices are pleasing to God" (13:16). Yes, here it is, this is the sacrifice worth saving: the sacrifice of praise, of doing good works and sharing what you have.

Think about the people who have defined sacrifice this way in our own lives: parents, teachers, friends, family members, doctors, military personnel. Think of people who have put doing good above all else, who may know the spiritual secret hidden in plain sight, that there is nothing to add or take away from the once-for-all sacrifice that has taken place in Christ. God transformed the cruelty of the cross into a supreme act of love—a love that inspires us to live as Christ did, not to die as he did. as Hebrews goes to great lengths to show us, that work has already been done for us.

Anne: Sacrifice—giving up something of value for something else—in and of itself, is not a bad thing. Jesus, after all, sacrificed all kinds of things in his life to live in "at-one-ment" with God. Jesus sacrificed popularity as he hung out with prostitutes, tax collectors, and other not-so-perfect people. But he did so to share God's love with others. Jesus sacrificed a stable home life as he traipsed around from town to town, sometimes sleeping on a boat, other times not sleeping at all. But he did so to share God's love with others. Jesus sacrificed a good reputation by healing on the Sabbath and talking to Samaritans. But he did so to share God's love. Jesus sacrificed his privacy and pride as he was stripped down, beaten, and hung naked to die. But all the while he was sharing the love of God with others, saying, "Father, forgive them, for they know not what they do" (Luke 23:24).

You see, when we talk about Jesus' sacrifice, we uually think only of his death, but there is so much more. Jesus was the Son of God for crying out loud! He could have done anything, been anything, and gone anywhere. But he sacrificed. His was *not* a lifestyle of the rich and famous. He didn't accept any roses from any suitors. He endured forty days in the wilderness on his own without any prize money at the end to show for it.

We use the word atonement to talk about Jesus dying for our sins, but atonement, or "at-one-ment" with God, is what Jesus showed us with his life. In that way, Jesus is like our VIP backstage pass to God's green room. Jesus allows us to meet and greet God in person. He allows us to see and experience God's love in ways that are tangible and understandable to us, rather than foreign, unfamiliar, and hidden. If the old covenant system kept God at a distance, the new covenant that is given to us in Jesus pulls God close. There is no longer a curtain between God and us. With Jesus as high priest, all of us as regular people get to take part in the priestly actions. We, the people, become priests, getting as close to God as we want.

But we have to want to get close to God. Sometimes we prefer to distance ourselves from God. We think it's too hard to believe in God or Jesus' once-for-all sacrifice because we're scientific, rational people, or because talking to God in prayer is a little too touchy-feely and we don't do talk therapy, thank you very much.

We don't just do this with God though. We do this with other people, too. We put up our own curtains and walls, protecting our "holy of holies," our hearts. We shy away from vulnerability, thinking that keeping ourselves closed off from others will protect us and keep us from getting hurt. In reality, it just creates more distance and hurts us.

You know the freedom you feel when you trust someone enough to drop the masks you wear and allow the walls around your heart to fall down? You're no longer exhausted, no longer faking it, no longer trying to pretend to be something you're not to impress somebody. You know that feeling? That's the feeling that God wants us to have with God, but we have to let those walls down. And Jesus shows us how to remove the curtain between us and God altogether by talking to people we do not know, taking risks, loving when it doesn't make sense, loving when it's inconvenient, loving when it means sacrificing something good for something better. Jesus is how we come to know God. Jesus is our VIP pass to God's green room, and we all get one of these passes—completely free of charge.

Andrew: Do you remember earlier when we talked about that secret (or not-so-secret) psychology of feeling like insiders, that powerful feeling of being in on the good stuff and not missing out on anything?

What about when it comes to life together in the church? As we learn from Hebrews, there is a vital difference between passive faith and passionate faith. The preacher is persuading the congregation to act on what they already know of Christ—remember they are theological insiders, here. But these are people who went from being living sacrifices (passionate faith) to becoming bystanders and onlookers in the faith (passive faith).

One way to think about this is by taking the Facebook phenomenon, for example. Some studies worry that Facebook could be making us lonelier, or more isolated, or jealous of all the seemingly perfect lives we see glimpses of on our feeds.

Here's the interesting thing: *This downside of Facebook seems to emerge mostly when we become passive viewers and not a part of the experience.* In other words, when we become "lurkers," or people who just hang out around the edges, so to speak, but never engage.

A 2010 study from Carnegie Mellon found that, when people engaged on Facebook, posting, messaging, liking, etc., their feelings of general social capital increased, while loneliness decreased. But when the study participants simply lurked, Facebook acted in the opposite way, increasing their sense of loneliness and isolation.[9]

According to researcher Moira Burke, lurking on Facebook correlates to an increase in depression. "If two women each talk to their friends the same amount of time, but one of them spends more time reading about friends on Facebook as well, the one reading tends to grow slightly more depressed," Burke says.[10]

It makes me wonder: how many "lurkers" around church do we have these days? What would it take to move us from a passive faith to a passionate faith?

If you are feeling more like an outsider these days, what would it take for you to accept God's invitation to the spiritual green room? If you're feeling disconnected from faith and God, maybe it's time to invest rather than pull back, to start a ministry team or lead a group, to give financially in a way that you never have before.

Or if you feel like you're expendable in this community, if you're feeling unheard, or if your tired and uninspired in your parenting or your profession or your relationships, maybe the way to feel connected is to jump in and lead. Maybe getting involved will help. Challenge yourself to make a commitment to attend worship as a living sacrifice of praise, of doing good and sharing what you have. Choose connectivity and see what it can do for your physical, mental, social, and spiritual health.

Anne: When it comes to our faith, Yale Professor Thomas Troeger gives us a strong reason to choose connectivity over isolation, passion over passivity: And we can choose connectivity over isolation, passion over passivity because of Christ.

The reality is, there's something in our human nature that leads us to point fingers at others and immediately try to find someone else to blame when things go wrong in life. We ask, "whose fault is it?" And we'll even go so far as to pin blame on someone even if they are innocent just so we can close that case and move on, so to speak. We like answers and we like justice, an eye for an eye. We like to even the score. God knows this about us and the author of Hebrews believes that Jesus meets this need of ours: "Christ has appeared once for all at the end of the age to remove sin by the sacrifice of himself" (Heb 9:26).

As Professor Troeger writes,

"Christ has died; now let that be the end of it. No more fixing the blame on each other. No more sacrificing innocents. No more doing each other in. Instead of spending your time arguing about who is at fault, spend your time "eagerly waiting" for Christ, and the way to eagerly wait for Christ is to get the world ready so that it will be a place fit for his arrival.

Give up the scapegoating and get to work. Christ is coming."[11]

Amen.

Notes

1. Mark S. Heim, *Saved from Sacrifice: A Theology of the Cross* (Cambridge: Eerdmans, 2006), 244.

2. Fred B. Craddock, "The Letter to the Hebrews: Introduction, Commentary, and Reflections," *The New Interpreter's Bible*, Volume XII, (Nashville, TN: Abingdon Press, 1998), 103–04.

3. Ibid, 110.

4. Heim, 244.

5. Roger Haight, *The Future of Christology* (New York: Continuum, 2005), 88.

6. Heim, 160.

7. Heim, 158.

8. Heim, 245.

9. Courtney Seiter, "The Secret Psychology of Facebook: Why we Like, Share, Comment, and Keep Coming Back," blog, April 23, 2015, https://blog.bufferapp.com/psychology-of-facebook (accessed July 25, 2015).

10. Ibid.

11. Thomas Troeger, "Preaching the Lesson II," https://www.goodpreacher.com/backissuesread.php?file=10100 (accessed July 23, 2015).

At-one-ment, Part Two: Accepting Forgiveness Once and for All

Hebrews 10:1-18

Traditional Christian theology teaches us that Jesus died on the cross for our sins. While this might be a familiar phrase of our faith, how compelling is this belief? Can Jesus' life and death really be compared to that of a bull being killed to make people feel better about themselves? Instead of understanding atonement as a theology of appeasing God by replacing our sin with Jesus' death, could it be that Jesus' death actually draws us to be "at one" with God's heart instead of fearing God's hate?

Andrew: The preacher of Hebrews is starting to sound a bit like a broken record, isn't he? If you've missed the past few weeks, today's text is a great recap: Jesus' death is a once-and-for-all sacrifice that puts a stop to the never-ending need for continual animal sacrifice, which was the norm in the Levitical priestly system of yore. For the past three chapters we've been steeped in priestly processes and protocols, learning that the blood of animals did nothing to change the hearts of people. This is why Jesus came to earth as our high priest—not just to die a bloody death, but to show us a life lived with love, a life that would transform our hearts with good and for good, not tax them with guilt for generation upon generation.

The verses cited above conclude what is called the "sermon within the sermon" of Hebrews (8:1–10:18), and the preacher goes out on a high note as he again quotes Jeremiah 31, the covenantal text on which this entire section is based. In this final stanza of his salvation song, the preacher reiterates two features of the Jeremiah covenant: its inward nature and that God remembers sin no more.[1] In essence, this new covenant aims to change lives from the inside out with a repeated: "In Jesus Christ you are forgiven."[2] Now this is good news, yes? It bears repeating, and it needs to be sung from the rooftops! "In Jesus Christ you are forgiven!" We are assured of pardon! But what does that mean?

Because all the scriptural material for today is a review of what we've already read and spoken on, we aren't going to review the biblical text verse by verse today. Rather, we're going to share with you some theological reflections on this Christian claim: "Jesus died on the cross for our sins." In other words, we're going to explore the meaning—or meanings—of "atonement," a theology that is meant to bring us more and more "at one" with God.

As we ping-pong back and forth through different voices and views of atonement throughout Christian history (and it will feel like a ping-pong match, so be prepared!), listen for the understanding or perspective that stirs your heart or that makes that light bulb go off in your head. Because in the end, like the popular children's book series of the '80s and '90s, this will be a "Choose Your Own Adventure"[3] type of thing. When it comes to theology, and especially atonement theology, there really is more choice in the matter than you might think.

Anne: First of all, what is "the atonement," and how has it been traditionally understood by Christianity at large? The English word "atonement" originally meant "at-one-ment", being "at one" or in harmony with someone.[4] In Western Christian theology, "atonement" came to describe how human beings are reconciled to God, referring to "the forgiving or pardoning of sin through the death and resurrection of Jesus."[5] Historically, there are a few lines of thought about how this happens.

One of the earliest explanations for how the atonement works is called the "moral influence theory," meaning, the core of Christianity is positive moral change, and the purpose of everything the Jewish Jesus did was to lead humans toward that moral change. He accomplished this moral change through his teachings, his example, and "the inspiring power of his martyrdom and resurrection."[6] In other words, Jesus was more martyr than savior. The "moral influence theory" is actually the oldest of the traditional views of atonement and was widely taught by the Church Fathers in the second and third centuries AD.[7]

The second traditional understanding of the atonement is the "Ransom" or "Christus Victor" theory, officially penned by St. Irenaeus in the second century.[8] In the "ransom" metaphor, Jesus—by giving his own life as a ransom sacrifice (Mt 20:28)—liberates humanity from the slavery of sin, from Satan, and thus ultimately from death. Victory over Satan consists of swapping the life of the perfect Jesus for the lives of us imperfect humans. In the "Christus Victor" theory, Jesus is not passively used as a ransom. Instead, Jesus himself actively defeats Satan in a literal spiritual battle, thus freeing us humans who were enslaved to the devil's sinful ways. These two different but related theories influenced Christian theology for about 1,000 years, until 1098 when the Benedictine monk and Catholic archbishop of Canterbury, St. Anselm, wrote his treatise, *Cur Deus Homo?*, which is Latin for, "Why did God become Human?"[9] Anselm sought to provide a rational argument for the necessity of the incarnation and death of Jesus, so he created the "satisfaction" or "payment for sin" theory. In this view, humanity owes a debt not to Satan, but to our sovereign, or supreme ruler, God.

How did he make this leap? Anselm used a cultural model drawn from his time and place: the relationship of a medieval lord to his peasants:

> If a peasant disobeyed the lord, could the lord simply forgive if he wanted to? No. Because that might imply that disobedience didn't matter that much. Instead, compensation must be made. Nothing less than the honor and order of the lord were at stake. Anselm applied that model to our relationship with God. We have been disobedient and deserve to be punished. And yet God loves us and wants to forgive us. But the price of sin must be paid. Jesus as a human being who was also divine and thus perfect and without sin [paid that price for us].[10]

Finally, the Reformers developed Anselm's theory even further into what has become the commonly held Protestant "penal substitution theory," which, instead of considering sin as an affront to God's honor, sees sin as the breaking of God's moral law.[11] Think of Romans 6:23: "the wages of sin is death." Penal substitution sees sinful man as being subject to God's wrath. The essence of Jesus' saving work is his substitution in the sinner's place, "bearing the curse in the place of man" (Gal 3:13). Whether you view sin as an affront to God's honor or to God's moral law, the point is: we should be the ones crucified for our sin. Instead, Jesus "paid it all" for us. No wonder so many Christians walk around feeling guilty and ashamed all the time!

Andrew: I'll be confessional with you: I am have done my fair share of reassessing and rethinking and reconsidering what I myself was taught as a child, namely, that Jesus died for me. I am just one of many Christians today who find it hard to accept Saint Anselm's quite genius idea (at the time anyway) that the penalty of human sin did damage to God's honor and that only the payment of Christ's death could make up for it. Even those powerful words "Jesus died for me" has many possible interpretations that are primarily taken from Paul's letters. In them, he uses a number of different images that speak of a transaction necessary to achieve salvation or salvation that comes about through penalty-bearing or redemption-purchasing.[12] These images, though, are essentially nowhere to be found in the Gospels.

Many more Christians today are searching for alternative ways to understand the deep meaning of Jesus' death, and as it turns out, there are indeed many different Christian responses to this. This is good news for those of us who are no longer convinced that God's sense of justice would demand the sacrifice of an innocent victim to gain forgiveness—for what kind of loving father would make forgiveness conditional on such a cruel and brutal act as the cross? Why would God have to be persuaded to love what God created?

Early creeds and confessions in the church had official views on important subjects like the incarnation (who Jesus was) and the Trinity (who God is), but there has never been any single, official formula on the meaning of Jesus' death. A brutal execution had become important, but the church had never applied an official meaning to it. Quite remarkable! Which is why, when it comes to the whole theological business of atonement, there can be lots of opinions about the significance and meaning of the cross without anyone being kicked out of the church because of it.

One prominent church example would be the Franciscans who emerged in the 13th century because they didn't believe that the traditional atonement theory said much good about God. They saw that God loved what he made. Therefore, there should never be any need for a transaction or a blood sacrifice or atonement of any kind. In the words of Franciscan John Duns Scotus, one of the most important philosopher-theologians of the Middle Ages, "Jesus did not come to change the mind of God about humanity, but to change the mind of humanity about God."[13]

Anne: Like the Franciscans of the Middle Ages, New Testament scholar Marcus Borg struggled with traditional atonement theology and worked to re-imagine the cross, acknowledging its centrality in the beginnings of Christianity and in the New Testament Scriptures.[14]

Borg saw the cross as primarily having a political meaning, arguing, "Jesus was executed by the authorities, and if we ask why, the most persuasive historical explanation is because of Jesus' passion for the Kin-dom of God, which involved him in radical criticism of the dominant system of his day. That system killed him, not God. The cross tells us what oppressive, dominant systems often do to those who oppose them."[15]

On a hopeful note, Borg espoused that the cross, post-resurrection, had a more personal and individual meaning as "a symbol or image for the path of transformation, for what it means to follow Jesus. . . . It means to die and rise with Christ. We find Paul saying the same: "I have been crucified with Christ. It is no longer I who live, but Christ who lives in me" (Gal 2:20). Here, the cross is an image for the path of spiritual and psychological transformation that leads to a new identity and way of being,"[16] following with one's whole heart, mind, soul, and body in the Way of Jesus.

Borg reminds us that the language of "Jesus as the once and for all sacrifice for sin" is actually a post-Easter interpretation of Jesus' death that emerges within the early Christian community. Understanding this context allows us to see that the cross is a proclamation of radical grace, not a tool for inflicting guilt. The connection is this: if Jesus is the "once and for all sacrifice for sin," understood metaphorically now by the post-Resurrection community of believers, that means that "God has already taken care of whatever it is that we think separates us from God. It means that God accepts us just as we are and that the Christian life is not about getting right with God. God's already taken care of that."[17] In other words, if you're going to think of Jesus' death as a sacrifice, then do it and be done with it! The point is not perpetual guilt, but forever forgiveness.

Andrew: In its own unmistakable way, chapters 9 and 10 of Hebrews are offering a response to the natural question: Why does Jesus' death matter? Or perhaps the more precise question being answered is, How does Jesus' death matter? Hebrews spells this out in these chapters with even greater detail than Paul's letters, all the while using the theology and language of sacrifice. Remember that Hebrews keeps drawing the comparison between the old and the new, between the old covenant where the high priest goes repeatedly into the Most Holy Place, "taking the blood that he offers for himself and for the sins committed unintentionally by the people" (9:22), and Christ's "sacrifice of himself" (9:26), which is a "once for all" action, his "single offering" (9:26; 10:14).

But remember from last week that this is not just a sacrifice for the sake of sacrifice. The sacrifice worth saving is the sacrifice of doing good and sharing what you have, according to Hebrews. And this is exactly what makes Jesus' sacrifice the perfect one. Jesus voluntarily became vulnerability for his whole life—not just the last three hours of his suffering and death that ended his life, but the three years of offering others the gift of God through his message that the kin-dom of God was among the people.

When Jesus' three years of traveling, teaching, and miracles end in Jerusalem on a Roman cross, his death is a culmination of the life that he lived. His execution amidst common thieves is his ultimate act of solidarity with every human being. We have all experienced godlessness and god-forsakenness, even Jesus in that moment. This is what made God designate Christ "a high priest according to the order of Melchizedek" (5:10). Jesus' character in life made the sacrifice of his death the "once for all" salvation for creation and humankind. Christ's moral solidarity with human beings gives more power to the proclamation "Jesus died for me," because he knows what it's like to suffer and be poor and marginalized.

Remember the sort of priest Hebrews describes Christ being, "In the days of his flesh, Jesus offered up prayers and supplications, with loud cries and tears, to the one who was able to save him from death, and he was heard because of his reverent submission" (5:7). It was God's solidarity with Jesus that made Jesus' solidarity with human beings so powerful that he became "the source of eternal salvation for all who obey him" (5:9). This is why his death matters so much, not because God required a sacrifice and Jesus performed the sacrifice, but rather because God was participating in human life through the life, death, and ultimate resurrection of Jesus.

With this in mind, theologian Mark Heim helps us understand the meaning of the cross and Jesus' death through the eyes of the poor and marginalized. He writes:

> The testimony of numberless such persons indicates that they do not see in the cross a mandate for passive suffering of evil. What they see, in the midst of a world that regards them as nobodies, is the most powerful

affirmation of their individual worth. That Christ, that God, was willing to suffer and die specifically for them is a message of hope and self-respect that can hardly be measured, and that transforms their lives. That God has become one of the broken and despised ones of history is an unshakable reference point from which to resist the mental colonization that accepts God as belonging to the side of the oppressors.[18]

Christ crucified means that all of those who have ever experienced godlessness, who have ever felt forsaken, who have ever been oppressed by enemies and the innocent victims of sinful systems that dehumanize and demoralize, are nevertheless loved, precious, and worthy. And Christ on the cross proves it so, not so much as a sacrifice, but as an act of solidarity with all who suffer.

Anne: Okay, we've heard enough about atonement from men. What do women have to say about this? Like Mark Heim, Dr. Pamela Cooper-White—the Professor of Pastoral Theology, Care, and Counseling at Columbia Theological Seminary—approaches the cross with an experienced and empathetic heart, unable to understand Jesus' death without somehow understanding that it speaks to how God suffers with and for us in the world. She says that the doctrine of Christ's crucifixion as atonement for Adam's fall (Gen 3:1-24) problematically "exalts suffering as redemptive,"[19] arguing:

> Feminist theologians critique this understanding as a glorification of suffering, repudiating the idea that suffering for its own sake is ever redemptive. The cross should not be interpreted to sanctify victimization, which reinforces submission to violence by women and other oppressed groups. Rather Jesus' [death] should be understood in liberationist terms as his refusal to back down in the face of oppression and evil, and his willingness to stand for healing, mercy, and justice for the least and the outcasts—even at the penalty of torture and death. Through Jesus, God's own self enters human suffering and the cross becomes a symbol of God's eternal solidarity with all who suffer.[20]

With this framework, Cooper-White asks, "What then can we discern about God's activity in the midst of suffering?" She answers reflectively,

> If suffering is more than sheer pain, but is the meaning made of pain, what alternative redemptive meanings can the cross have? A liberationist theology of the cross understands God's solidarity with human suffering as an expression of God's ultimate receiving of the creature's pain and suffering into God's own being. Healing and salvation is the recognition of our cry of suffering, even the incarnate, embodied receiving of our pain as God's pain, and through this recognition and receiving, the transformation of our pain into new life. . . . The resurrection becomes a sign of the new life that is possible beyond both pain and suffering, a redemption not only or primarily from sin, stain, or fault, but from all creaturely grief, victimization, and affliction.[21]

For Cooper-White, and perhaps for some of us, the cross is the singular event in Jesus' life that helps us know and truly believe that we are not alone in our suffering, that God understands our pain and hurts with us and for us, and that suffering never gets the last word; transformation does.

Andrew: Trying to understand what the cross really means has become a sort of theological piñata. Every person takes a crack at what the death of Jesus means, and nothing really sticks once and for all. Remember, there never was a single, official formula on the meaning of Jesus' death. Which is why we have multiple meanings and interpretations supplied by a whole host of theologians and spiritual thinkers.

After all, atonement is trying to explain what salvation means in the life and death and resurrection of Jesus and how that salvation comes about.

Roger Haight, a Jesuit theologian at Union Seminary NY, offers a helpful general conception of salvation, saying, "Salvation may be understood as a condition of being united with God, and in and through God a being united with other human beings and at peace in one's existence."[22]

This definition complements the Latin word *salvus* from which we get our word salvation. *Salvus* means "heal and whole." You can hear the word "salve" in there, too, like a salve for a wound. To be united to God and to others is to be complete. To experience oneness and wholeness allows our way of being to coincide with God's way of being as seen in the life of Jesus.

Salvation in these terms is good news: unity with God; unity through God with others. Peace in one's existence. Healing. Wholeness.

This substance of salvation is a bit of a contrast to the multiple metaphors and analogies and images that have been associated with salvation, like paying a ransom, using Jesus as a scapegoat, and making satisfaction for sin. The Christian tradition has supplied all of these views as different ways we might come to understand Jesus as Savior.

Again, Roger Haight says that, apart from these metaphors, there is another way to think of God's salvation in Jesus: as a "revealer" of God's salvation. He says, "What has been revealed to Christians in the ministry, death, and resurrection of Jesus regards the very nature of God as savior. But this means that God has always been savior and that salvation has been going on since 'the beginning.' There never was a time when God was not savior, nor a period in human history when God's salvation was ineffective."[23] Jesus' life, then, is a "parable of God's salvation" that has been ongoing since before the prophet Isaiah's words, "Do not fear, for I have redeemed you; I have called you by name, and you are mine . . . I am the Lord your God, the Holy One of Israel, your Savior . . . Do not fear, for I am with you . . . I will bring my sons from far away and my daughters from the end of the earth . . . everyone . . . whom I created for my glory, whom I formed and made" (43:1, 3; 41:10; 43:6, 7).

The reach of Isaiah's vision was not for the sake of Israel only, but for that of the world. That's why the prophet can so boldly announce in Isaiah 19, "In that day there will be an altar to the Lord in the heart of Egypt, and an altar to the Lord at its border. It will be a sign and a witness to the Lord of hosts in the land of Egypt; when they cry to the Lord because of oppressors, he will send them a savior, and will defend and deliver them" (vv. 19-20). Egypt is Israel's enemy. Hated. Despised. Isaiah reveals that the ones far away will be brought near; the ones facing condemnation will be restored. From creation to Christ, God's salvation is more expansive than we ever dreamed.

Anne: Is your mind expanded to point of bursting? We've just taken you on a theological rollercoaster—a chance to "Choose Your Own Adventure" theologically. What's most important about our faith is that it is alive and adventurous and not stale, stalled out, or stuck in cynicism. If we are stopped in our tracks by a theological belief that creates distance between us and God, then chances are—as the preacher of Hebrews is telling his own people—that belief or theology is not helping us live into the Jeremiah 31 covenant. If a specific theological understanding of the atonement (or anything for that matter) is keeping us from having God's love carved into our hearts and engraved into our minds, then it is not serving to strengthen our relationship with God. That was the main purpose of Jesus coming as our Great High Priest, and it remains the main purpose of Jesus' incarnational love in our lives today.

All that said, which of these understandings speaks to you? Which one helps you understand God's radical love, forgiveness, and grace in your life? Whatever understanding of the atonement you're drawn to is an understanding worth holding onto for dear life! Theology, by its very nature, is messy, not clear-cut. Theology is, after all, the study of God. The author of Hebrews is driving home the point that Jesus came to earth to de-mystify God a bit for us. Instead of letting certain beliefs about Jesus' life and death become iron-clad truth in our minds and teachings, it might serve us better to see Jesus' life and death and resurrection as invitations to journey deeper into the mystery of God.

What meaning (or meanings) of the "atonement" brings you the closest to being "at one" with God? There is no one right answer. No matter what you believe, the Table is where we enact our faith, where we remember Jesus' love. The Table is what draws us, again and again, to be "at one" with God and with one another.

Andrew: It might come as a surprise to some that the cross was not an important visual symbol for the early church: we have no visual images of the cross or crucifixion from the first three to four centuries of church history. At that time Jesus was depicted as the good shepherd, the healer of a blind man or a paralytic man, but not as suffering.

And when it comes to what matters most to God, even Jesus talks about receiving the kin-dom of God as a little child (Lk 18:17). However we think about the meaning of the cross and Jesus' death, and whatever theory of atonement we might believe in, Scripture reminds again and again that we don't have anything to fear. We never need to be distracted or to stray far from the gospel message of "fear not." Which is why it's good to know that when we read a book like Hebrews and seek to understand what sacrifice means or what atonement means, we read these through the lens of the Gospels. And if we listen long enough to Jesus, we find out that experiencing grace and entering the kin-dom of God is done through the sort of honesty and receptivity that we see in a child. The truth is,

> none of this death-centered salvation occurs in the sayings and deeds of Jesus. The gospels indicate that a constant stream of people came to him for spiritual aid, and he extended God's forgiveness, healing and salvation to them (long before he ever died!). Without any reference to

atonement, redemption, or a substitutionary death, Jesus affirms that goodness comes from good motivation, that people can do the will of God, can practice mercy, justice, honesty and trust. He emphasizes God's desire to seek out and save the lost, to give good things to his children, to throw open the doors of the kin-dom to those who really want to enter.[24]

Amen.

Notes

1. Fred B. Craddock, "The Letter to the Hebrews: Introduction, Commentary, and Reflections" *The New Interpreter's Bible*, Volume XII, (Nashville, TN: Abingdon Press, 1998), 116.

2. Thomas G. Long, *Hebrews: Interpretation: A Bible Commentary for Teaching and Preaching* (Louisville: John Knox Press, 1997), 101.

3. *Choose Your Own Adventures* (a concept created by Edward Packard) is a young adult novel series where at the end of every chapter the reader decides what happens next. If the reader chooses option A, they jump to the indicated page number; if the reader chooses option B, they jump to a different page number. In this way, the reader has agency in determining how the story ends. The books can be read multiple times with different outcomes as the reader chooses different options.

4. Niels-erik A. Andreasen, "Atonement/Expiation in the Old Testament," W. E. Mills, ed., *Mercer Dictionary of the Bible* (Mercer University Press, 1990).

5. Definitions of atonement, http://www.merriam-webster.com/dictionary/atonement (accessed August 2, 2015); http://www.collinsdictionary.com/dictionary/english/atonement?showCookiePolicy=true (accessed August 2, 2015).

6. A. J. Wallace, R. D. Rusk, *Moral Transformation: The Original Christian Paradigm of Salvation* (New Zealand: Bridgehead, 2011).

7. This view also enjoyed popularity in the Middle Ages and is espoused by later philosophers and theologians like Immanuel Kant and Paul Tillich.

8. H. N. Oxenham, *The Catholic Doctrine of the Atonement*, xliv, (London: Longman, Green, Longman, Roberts, and Green, 1865), 114.

9. Ibid., 114

10. Ibid.

11. Vincent Taylor, *The Cross of Christ* (London: Macmillan & Co, 1956), 71-2; L. W. Grensted, *A Short History of the Doctrine of the Atonement*, (Manchester: Manchester University Press, 1920), 191.

12. Stephen Finlan, *Options on Atonement in Christian Thought* (Collegeville: Liturgical Press, 2007), 3.

13. Richard Rohr, *Embracing an Alternative Orthodoxy* (Denver: Church Publishing Incorporated, 2014), 14–15.

14. In one of his earliest letters in the '50s, Paul summarized "the gospel" he had taught to his community in Corinth as "Christ crucified" (I Cor. 1-2). And in all four gospels, the story of Jesus' final week and its climax in the crucifixion and resurrection dominates the narrative, the last week of Jesus' life taking up more than a fourth of each text. And, Borg says, all four gospel writers anticipate the end of Jesus' life earlier in their narratives. It is as if they are saying: you can't tell the story of Jesus unless you tell the story of the cross. But the questions remain about the cross: What does it mean? Why does it matter? What is its significance?" Marcus Borg, "Christianity Divided by the Cross," *Patheos.com*, Oct 25, 2013, http://www.patheos.com/blogs/marcusborg/2013/10/christianity-divided-by-the-cross/ (accessed August 1, 2015); Marcus Borg, "Christianity Divided by the Cross" *Patheos.com*, October 25, 2013, http://www.patheos.com/blogs/marcusborg/2013/10/christianity-divided-by-the-cross/ (accessed August 1, 2015).

15. Marcus Borg, "What is the Significance of the Cross and the Crucifixion of Jesus" *Explorefaith.org*, http://www.explorefaith.org/questions/cross.html (accessed August 1, 2015).

16. Ibid.

17. Ibid.

18. Mark Heim, "Why Does Jesus Death Matter?," *The Christian Century*, March 7, 2001, 12–17.

19. Pamela Cooper-White, "Suffering" in *The Wiley Blackwell Companion to Practical Theology*, ed. Bonnie J. Miller-McLemore (Malden, MA: Blackwell Publishing Limited, 2012), 28.

20. Ibid., 28.

21. Ibid., 28-29.

22. Roger Haight, *The Future of Christology* (New York: Continuum, 2005), 90.

23. Ibid, 91.

24. Finlan, 35.

12

Whole-hearted Faith

Hebrews 10:19-38

Since the days of the early Christians, following God in the way of Jesus has never been an easy road. In fact, the opposite is true then and now. A living faith that stands the test of time requires courage to face challenges of all kinds. We will suffer loss, we will risk ridicule and danger, there will be much we won't understand, we might get hurt, and we will need to make sacrifices that we'd rather not make. Sometimes it's hard to have the patience to push past our pain in the present moment to live with confidence and hope that God promises a good future that we can't yet see. What makes for a full-hearted faith? And is it worth it? What makes it worth it? See why "when the 'stuff' hits the fan" in our faith, it's not the time to lose heart. It is the time to keep hope alive by putting our whole hearts into it.

Andrew: *The Daily Show with Jon Stewart*, and now with Trevor Noah, connected with younger generations who are tired and uninspired by the politicizing of religion and the religionizing of politics in America. Through disarming humor, calling out hot air and hypocrisy, and speaking to the issues of our time with a healthy dose of satire and truth-telling irreverence, *The Daily Show's* audiences happen to be those "perfectly aligned with those absent from many churches."[1]

After Church had this to say about the first host, "Jon Stewart has been one of the most regular and consistent provocateurs of moral thinking on contemporary topics with a level of thoughtfulness, complexity, and sincerity absent in much preaching today."[2]

There it is. Thoughtfulness. Complexity. Sincerity. You don't have to believe that Jon Stewart is America's pastor to see that this was the way he delivered the news. It's a pretty good way to describe how the pastor in Hebrews delivers the good news, too.

If you've been around for the last couple of weeks, you may recall that the last three and a half chapters in Hebrews has been one long "preacherly" monologue about the meaning of Jesus' sacrifice and his identity as a high priest. The writer of Hebrews obviously has a scholar's mind and a pastor's heart, having led us through a theological gauntlet of who Christ is for the salvation of human beings.

Today's text turns our attention to more practical matters, like, "What do we do about what we have heard?" I mean, think about being a first-time listener to the longest sermon in the New Testament and hearing this charge: "Therefore, my friends . . . hold fast to the confession of our hope without wavering, for he who has promised is faithful. And let us consider how to provoke one another to love and good deeds, not neglecting to meet together, as is the habit of some, but encouraging one another . . ." (10:19a, 23-25a).

Let's stop right there to say that, if you want a good working definition for the gospel, it is right here in Hebrews: Cheer each other on in order to fulfill love and good deeds. Worship together and don't neglect it like so many are doing. Encourage one another. All of the thoughtfulness and complexity that we have heard is now lived out with sincerity of heart and actions.

But what difference does any of this make in the way we live our lives?

It's important to keep in mind that some "stuff had hit the fan" in the lives of these listeners. The preacher is reminding the people of their past—"coaching them up" so to speak about how confident and compassionate and steadfast amidst suffering that they had been. The preacher encourages them to,

> . . . recall those earlier days when, after you had been enlightened, you endured a hard struggle with sufferings, sometimes being publicly exposed to abuse and persecution, and sometimes being partners with those so treated. For you had compassion for those who were in prison, and you cheerfully accepted the plundering of your possessions, knowing that you yourselves possessed something better and more lasting. (10:32-34)

This is a picture of perseverance for those who endured pain in very public ways. After they "had been enlightened" and joined the Jesus movement, they went through "a hard struggle with sufferings" (v. 32). They suffered violence—both verbal and physical. They were put in prison.

Their empty homes were looted and burglarized. This was no hypothetical or theoretical matter.³

Now the preacher is reminding them of those early days in the faith when they were brave and bold and did not back down. A time when their hearts were not hardened by their hardships. A time when they risked losing their possessions, because they possessed a reward that could never be taken away. They "possessed something better and more lasting" (v. 34). But now, rather than having the kind of whole-hearted faith that had inspired them to "compassion for those who were in prison" and "cheerfully accepting the plundering of possessions" and living with a confidence that would bring a great reward (10:34-35), they were now giving up on the grace of God they had experienced. They had even stopped worshiping together. Even worse than no longer *going* to church, they had stopped *being* the church. Instead of exhibiting courage and compassion in their faith, they were cowardly and cold. The preacher of Hebrews puts it hardest and harshest of all, chastising them for belittling the Son of God and shaming and mistreating the "Spirit of grace" (v. 29). Before he seems to slam the spiritual door in their faces, the preacher of Hebrews clenches his jaw and quotes Scripture to clinch his point: "Vengeance belongs to God . . . The Lord will judge his people" (v. 30).

The congregation's once whole-hearted faith now has a lot of holes in it—shot through by sin and suffering pain that only God fully knows. And the preacher is pleading with them to not reject the truth they once knew, not to give up on being the church. He implores them to put their whole hearts into it again. The teacher of preachers, Tom Long, uses a Colorado kind of analogy to explain what Hebrews means here, saying, "The Preacher's congregation is like a group of imperiled rock climbers who are being pulled to safety by the rope of faith. Just as they are nearing the top of the rock face, they have decided that they are growing tired and they just might let go of the rope. No wonder the preacher screams out a warning, 'If you let go, there is no saving you'."⁴

I have to admit that I have sympathy for the congregation of Hebrews. Let's face it: they had been persecuted for their faith. We don't really know what that's like in the United States. Some Christians suffer from what one writer calls "CPC—the Christian persecution complex." They are Christians who want to force their faith onto others and use our political system to control the lives and behaviors of people who don't believe and live by the Bible. They believe that the Bible and not the Constitution should be the foundational document of our nation.

Well, Protestant privilege dies hard, and just because our faith may not be as popular as it once was does not mean that we are being persecuted for it. There is an infinite qualitative difference between real persecution and being disappointed that our religious beliefs don't get preferential treatment in our political democracy. The congregation in Hebrews knew what real persecution was about in some of the ways that Christians around the globe today are suffering real persecution. Author and former pastor Benjamin Dixon helps us understand this context, writing, "In North Korea, Christians can be executed for gathering together for worship. In Iraq, Christians are prey for terrorist groups that kill anyone who does not bow down to their particular version of Islam. In February of 2015, twenty-one Coptic Christians were beheaded simply because they were Christian. Reports indicate that many of them called on the name of Jesus just before they were viciously murdered. Persecution watchdog group Open Doors has identified fifty of the most dangerous places in the world for Christianity, in which believers suffer a range of tribulations from "severe" persecution to "sparse" persecution. The United States is not on the list.[5]

Even so, we may not be persecuted for our faith like the congregation in Hebrews or like Christians in other parts of the world today, but we are still full of conflict—not on the outside like the congregation in Hebrews but on the inside. Whether it is inside of ourselves or inside the Church itself, it's hard to know sometimes whether to stay in the race or get out.

I think for many people today, there is a "why bother" mentality about church. Some of us in this room struggle to understand why continuing in ours matters. We identify with those in the congregation in Hebrews who habitually "neglect to meet together." We understand how people might get tired in worship or tired of worship and lose focus, lose heart, and lose interest. If we happen to be burned out on going to church or being the church (like our spiritual ancestors in the book of Hebrews), then by "shrinking back" from church we know that nobody is going to ask us to serve on a committee or give money or lead a small group.

This week I read an article by someone else who sympathizes with such things about church. She says that she is trying to talk to "the Skeptics, the Cynics, the Critics; the Dones, the Nones . . . " when she writes:

> I hear you. You're my people. I see every bit of the drama, the pettiness, the poor stewardship, the moral grandstanding, the lack of authenticity and the love of tedious-meeting-having that defines westernized Christianity. I know it can be gross. I know. I know the music can be

bad, and the utility bill is higher than the mission giving. I know that sometimes the coffee is cold, and the styrofoam cups are killing us all. I know that we are embarrassingly late to the party on marriage equality, racial reconciliation and women's rights. I know that tri-fold brochures don't really change the world; that a Hallmark, fluffy cloud CareBear heaven is nothing to shape your whole life around; and that a cartoon devil with a pitchfork does not inspire spiritual growth. I know. You are right about every bit of it, and I feel your pain/boredom/disdain. It is all justified. And yet. I am still here.[6]

And it appears that you and I are still here, too, at least for now. Why is that, do you think? Why are you still here when so many are a hair-width away from becoming one of the so-called "dones," people with years of devotion to Christ and the church who have given up and are now "done"?

As this writer says, many of us have attachments to church life because they make us feel safe and comfortable. It might be about singing hymns or the feel of a sanctuary or the smell of a potluck meal or the thrill of going to a bunch of meetings (just kidding, sort of). If we learn anything from Hebrews, it's that such trappings do not make for a whole-hearted faith. There must be something more that is about transformation—the transformation of our relationships and ourselves. The deep-seated curiosity and hunger leads us to learn more about the "stuff" that Jesus says, like:

1. Love your neighbor as yourself.
2. Feed my sheep.
3. Go and make disciples.
4. Follow me.
5. Pray for your enemies.
6. Give to the poor.
7. Take. Eat. Remember.[7]

I happen to believe, with as much of my heart as I can, that there is no other community than the church that can teach us these things, not even *The Daily Show*. Sure, "Maybe his text is politics; his rituals, comedy; his vestments, American media—but the gospel, is an old and universal one. Be honest. Be kind. Have faith. Say thank you."[8]

That's a great start, but the truth is that if we get those other things right, then the world will be more peaceful, more compassionate. Truth and beauty and goodness and wisdom will rule the world. God knows (and Hebrews tells us so) that the church is not always living up to our definition of the Gospel. We are not—sincerely and with our whole hearts—being cheerleaders for one another to love and do good deeds. We aren't worshiping together or encouraging one another.

What does it means to "hold fast to the confession of our hope" (10:23)? What keeps our hearts from being "all in" and a powerful person of a whole-hearted faith? What keeps us from being a church that is compassionate and encouraging, risking vulnerability and worshiping together, and thereby transforming into the likeness of the One who is the image of the invisible God.

Can you feel that now is not the time to lose heart? What if now is the time to keep hope alive by putting our whole hearts into those meaningful relationships with which we are struggling? It might be time to put our whole heart into a relationship with our spouse or our partner or our children or our work or the work of the church.

Someone once said: "inside every person is a tragedy and a comedy and a masterpiece." The church needs to be a big enough place for everyone who is holding all of this in their hearts. At the same time, the church needs to hold fast to the confession of our hope that calls us toward a love that will never let us go and a place where we can finally be at home within ourselves, each other, and the deep and abiding love of God. We must say with our whole hearts, "Hear my cry, hear my call / Hold my hand lest I fall / Take my hand, precious Lord, lead me Home."[9]

Amen.

Notes

1. Patrick Scriven, "The Imminent Transition of Jon Stewart, America's Pastor," *After Church*, August 5, 2015, http://after.church/the-imminent-transition-of-jon-stewart-americas-pastor/ (accessed August 8, 2015).

2. Ibid.

3. Fred B. Craddock, "The Letter to the Hebrews: Introduction, Commentary, and Reflections" *The New Interpreter's Bible*, Volume XII, (Nashville, TN: Abingdon Press, 1998), 115.

4. Thomas G. Long, *Hebrews: Interpretation: A Bible Commentary for Teaching and Preaching* (Louisville: John Knox Press, 1997), 107.

5. Benjamin Dixon, "Please Stop with the Christian Persecution Complex. You're Embarrassing the Faith," *Patheos*, July 9, 2015, http://www.patheos.

com/blogs/godisnotarepublican/2015/07/please-stop-with-the-christian-persecution-complex-youre-embarrassing-the-faith/ (accessed August 7, 2015).

6. Erin Wathen, "$H*! Jesus Says: 7 Reasons I'm (Still) a Christian," *Patheos*, August 5, 2015, http://www.patheos.com/blogs/irreverin/2015/08/h-jesus-says-7-reasons-im-still-a-christian/ (accessed August 7, 2015).

7. Ibid.

8. Sonia Saraiya, "In the religion of calling bullsh*t, Jon Stewart was both preacher and disciple: 'If you smell something, say something'," *Salon*, August 7, 2015, http://www.salon.com/2015/08/07/if_you_smell_something_say_something_with_a_final_inspirational_sermon_jon_stewart_bids_a_fitting_farewell_to_the_daily_show/ (accessed August 8, 2015).

9. Booth Brothers, "Take My Hand Precious Lord," lyrics, https://boothbrothers.com/song/take-my-hand-precious-lord/.

13

The Fantasy that Faith Requires

Hebrews 10:39–11

"Now faith is the assurance of things hoped for, the conviction of things not seen," (v. 1). Hebrews 11 provides us with a litany of stories about people whose lives back up this oft-cited, cliché-ified verse with real, raw experience. The fact is, faith requires a fantastical mind and a flourishing, fanciful heart. We often seem to outgrow fantasies when we outgrow childhood, but this lack of imagination hinders us in our faith. It sets us up for an inability to believe that dreams come true and the good guy wins. But what is the kin-dom of God if it is not one fantastically beautiful dream where justice flows like the chocolate in Willy Wonka's Chocolate Factory and loving our neighbor is as easy as the tap of a magic wand? See what happens when we shelve our scientific mind for a bit (heaven forbid) and step into the wardrobe of wonder, allowing ourselves to have hope like a child that God's promises really can come true.

Anne: Back in the old country, there was a rabbi who invested his life savings in timber. When a forest fire broke out and his finances literally went up in smoke, the rabbi's friends worried about how to break the devastating news to him. They hemmed and hawed until the rabbi said, "You're afraid to tell me about the fire, aren't you?"

"You know?" they asked, surprised.

"I found out about an hour ago," he said.

"And you're not upset?" they asked.

"I was," he answered. "I'm over it now."

"It was only an hour ago!" they exclaimed.

"Tell me," the rabbi said to one of the men, "didn't you once suffer a loss by fire? Why aren't you distraught about it?"

"My fire was 10 years ago," he replied.

"Okay," the rabbi said, "so for you it took 10 years. For me it took an hour. The point is we both got over it."[1]

Rabbi Shais Taub, an American Hasidic Jew who is well known for his work with Jewish spirituality and 12-step addiction programs, tells this Jewish parable of sorts:

> One of life's great truths is that pain + time = healing. It's not the passage of time itself that heals; it's the perspective that time brings. The longer we live, the more experiences we have and the bigger our world becomes. With perspective, every hurt shrinks to a more manageable size. So the real formula seems to be pain + perspective = healing. If we could get perspective without time, that would work, too. It's just that, usually, we need to live longer before we can see things differently. But imagine what it would be like to have immediate perspective. What if we didn't have to wait for context to come?
>
> Is it possible to gain a perspective that allows us to contextualize the events of our lives in real time instead of having to wait until we can make a withdrawal from that emotional 401k called hindsight? Is there such thing as the ability to become a "quick healer" from the bangs and bruises of life? . . . The answer is "yes," . . . it's called faith.[2]

Faith, or *pistis* in the Greek, has "had a checkered past in the culture of the early church. In Greek mythology, Pistis was one of the spirits who escaped Pandora's box and fled back to heaven, abandoning humanity. In Luke's Gospel, for example, when Jesus wonders, 'Will the Son of Man find faith on earth?' (Luke 18:8), he was speaking to a Hellenistic culture that believed the spirit of Pistis [of faith] had already left."[3] The preacher of Hebrews wants to dismiss such dismal notions of a world abandoned by faith and encourage his listeners who (we all know by now) were Christians having trouble holding onto hope when Christ did not return immediately following the resurrection.[4]

Not only were they disappointed about Christ being a "no show" in their lives, but "some had been subjected to prison and plunder of possessions, and most had experienced hostility, ridicule, and shame, simply because following Jesus, a crucified savior, set them at odds with the surrounding culture."[5] After reminding them of the pain of their past, the preacher says as whole-heartedly as he can to his people, "*My friends*, we are not those who give up hope and so are lost; but we are of the company who live by faith and so are saved" (10:39, The Voice).

Our passage today consists of the 40 verses of Hebrews 11 known as the "Hall of Fame of Faith."[6] The Apostle Paul said "we walk by faith, not by sight" (2 Cor 5:7), yet as the preacher of Hebrews takes us on a walk through the hallways of biblical history, we actually see the story of our faith unfolding before us person by person, decision by decision. If the heart of Hebrews is hope, the hardiness of the Hebrew people is faith.

Do you remember how this whole sermon of Hebrews began? "Long ago God spoke to our ancestors in many and various ways . . . " (1:1). Well, now we know how our ancestors responded to the many and various ways God spoke to them—with faith: "Now faith is the assurance of things hoped for, the conviction of things not seen" (v. 1). This is how the preacher of Hebrews wants his people to respond to the highs and lows of their lives, the knowns and unknowns, the struggles and successes—with baby steps of faith on some days and giant leaps of faith on others. And this is how this preacher (me) wants her people to respond as well.

"We are of the company who live by faith" (10:39, The Voice). What company? According to biblical scholars, the company of the faithful listed in Hebrews 11 can be divided into four main categories: those who were righteous, those who journeyed obediently in faith, those who were tested by suffering, and those who were a mix of all of the above.[7]

"We are of the company who live by faith." We are of the company of Abel, Enoch, and Noah who lived by faith simply because they were righteous and pleasing to God. We know nothing of Abel's faith, but we assume God approved of him because God accepted his sacrifice and not Cain's.[8] According to Hebrews 11, simply having God's approval is a mark of faith (v. 2), and "without faith it is impossible to please God" (v. 6).

We know about as much about Enoch as we know about King Melchizedek, maybe less. Genesis 5:24 says, "Enoch walked with God; then he was no more, because God took him." Again, we know nothing of Enoch's faith from our Scriptures,[9] but the preacher infers that however Enoch walked with God it was pleasing enough for him to be taken directly to heaven without passing through death's door like the rest of us.[10]

Then there's Noah. God told Noah something crazy: that despite the fact that the sun was shining and the weather forecast was favorable, it was going to start raining, and the earth would be flooded, and Noah needed to build a huge ark to save his family. Noah had a choice: he could dismiss the voice he'd heard and trust what he saw in the world around him and his past experience of rain. Or he could listen to the voice he'd heard, trust that it was the voice of God, and do what God said. We all know what Noah chose. He built the ark and brought those animals on two by two! He too is remembered as a man of faith because of his righteous obedience to God.[11] He listened to God, believed what God said, and did what God told him to do.

"We are of the company who live by faith." We are of the company of Abraham and Sarah, Isaac, and Jacob, who lived by faith because they journeyed obediently with God. Abraham was "called to set out for a place that he was to receive as an inheritance" (v. 8), uprooting his family for generations, living as a permanent exile in a foreign land (v. 13), journeying God-knows-how far to a place he had never been or heard of or even knew existed! Sarah, then Isaac, then Jacob were all dragged along for the ride in one way or another. All of them journeyed to a land they were promised but never saw because they died before they arrived.[12] Their story of this multi-generational family of faith is one of believing in that which you cannot see and seeking it out whole-heartedly anyway, even when you have no idea where you're going, how you'll get there, or if your life will even be better once if you arrive on the other side—*if* you ever even arrive on the other side!

"We are of the company who live by faith." We are of the company of Abraham, Isaac, Jacob, Joseph, and Moses, who lived by faith because they were tested by suffering. While suffering can seem meaningless when you're stuck in the middle of it, these folks endured because they believed in a greater purpose of God that they could not see or understand. They believed in a "bigger picture," we might say. So much so that when Abraham was asked to sacrifice his own son, he actually began to do it, until God provided a ram.

Then there's the suffering that comes with death—of not being able to see the completion of what you've begun, of not being able to experience the love of the legacy you are leaving behind. Upon his deathbed, Isaac invoked blessings for his sons, unable to see them into their futures himself. Upon Jacob's deathbed, Jacob blessed each of the sons of his son, Joseph, unable to see them into their futures himself. Upon Joseph's deathbed, he spoke of the exodus of the Israelites, something which he did not see or experience himself but believed with his whole heart would happen, so much so that he wanted everyone around him to know about it before he died.[13]

And then there was Moses. Moses suffered a hard life from the beginning as a baby in a basket. He could have had the royal life but claimed for himself the call God gave him as a leader of God's chosen people in Egypt. His stuttering and self-doubt, as well as the plagues God sent upon Egypt, tried Moses. Finally he led God's people through the Red Sea, from slavery to freedom, only to get to the other side and deal with the people's long-suffering and never-ceasing complaints! It's easy to discard hope and discount faith when you are suffering, but these men endured.

"We are of the company who live by faith" (10:39). We are of the company of Rahab, Gideon, Barak, Samson, Jephthah, David, Samuel, the prophets and hosts of others, who lived by a faith through which they "received spies in peace, conquered kingdoms, administered justice, obtained promises, shut the mouths of lions, quenched raging fire, escaped the edge of the sword, won strength out of weakness, became mighty in war, put foreign armies to flight, were tortured, refused to accept release, suffered mocking and flogging, chains and imprisonment, were stoned to death, sawn in two, killed by the sword, who went about in skins of sheep and goats, destitute, persecuted, tormented, who wandered in deserts, mountains, in caves and holes in the ground" (11:31-38). Their lives are remembered as faithful because they used power properly, accepted victory with humility, and saw suffering as inevitable. Suffering wasn't seen as punishment; it was just part of living with faith.

How does your portrait of faith, your spiritual CV, look next to all these folks in Hebrew's "Faith Hall of Fame"? Perhaps less dramatic, but just as faithful. Or perhaps just as dramatic, but not as faithful. One pastor has speculated, "At the core of every person's religion is his or her own evaluation of their faith. Even if a person chooses not to believe the existence of God, their unbelief still encompasses a body of faith that is sustained by belief without seeing. As human beings, our lives are governed by the unseen that is associated with the possibilities of projected events. We are always seeking to advance and evolve socially, economically and, more importantly, spiritually. It is the projections of the things hoped for, or the future vision of a better quality of life, that stimulates our motivation to keep moving forward . . . it is in that future gazing that we must reconcile within us: is [this stuff] in our faith or is it just a fantasy we have projected in our minds?"[14]

Generations of Christians have come up with all kinds of excuses about how faith doesn't make sense to any reasonable person with a rational mind, or why faith is too hard live by, let alone believe in, or why our faith seems to let us down more than it lifts us up, or why having faith is just living in a child's make believe land and that kind of fantasy belief can't and won't make a difference in our lives.

But it does. Faith does make a difference, even if it is a bit fantastical. That's the point. Faith brings you into a world that you can't see on your own: a world that only God can see, but that you and I have to live in. *We have to make-believe a bit in order for us to believe at all.* We're good at this as kids. We love Disney princesses so much that we dress up as them and pretend their lives are our lives: believing that dragons die, and the good person always wins. We allow ourselves to really feel the wonder of Charlie when he first walks into Willy Wonka's Chocolate Factory, wishing we could be there too, having our own dreams come true with the luck of a golden ticket! You see? Fantasy allows us to have a perspective that we wouldn't have otherwise.

Listen again to Rabbi Taub, who muses:

> What is faith but the ability to sense that there is a reality that lies beyond the horizon of the intellect's farthest gaze? This is precisely why faith, by definition, can only properly begin once critical thinking has run smack up against its outermost limits.
>
> Accepting on faith that which can be understood is as unconscionable as using reason to reject something that cannot be understood. The former is laziness, the latter is arrogance. Both are predicated on the misconception rampant among fundamentalist believers and atheists alike that faith and intellect can somehow be used to perform the same function and that the one you choose to favor shows what kind of person you are, as if this were an argument over whether it's better to use a 7-wood or a 3-iron for a chip shot.
>
> Faith is no more interchangeable with intellect than breathing is a substitute for eating. We need both, but we cannot replace one with the other . . . With faith, our universe instantly expands, we become smaller and so do our troubles.[15]

Though faith has an element of fantasy to it, there is an importance distinction between the two:

> Fantasy is an idea we cling to in order to escape reality. Faith is an idea we cling to in order to have that courage to face [our reality] . . . This is the same difference that there is between 'getting out of yourself' and 'getting over yourself.' People use all types of distractions to 'get out of themselves'—drugs, relationships, sports, religiosity, gossip. These pastimes give us a way to check out of our real lives . . . At the end of the day, however, when the distracting activities cease, we still have to go back to our own consciousness. In contrast, 'getting over yourself' is a truly spiritual skill that entails taking yourself less seriously so that you can fully engage in reality without the need for the buffer of self-stimulation. When you get over yourself, you can experience whatever life has to offer at any given moment, even when it hurts . . . Being spiritual means having a big enough reality to absorb whatever temporary pain life may bring.[16]

Having faith is what helps us do that, and sometimes a bit of fantasy helps us get there.

In his book, *Good to Great*, author Jim Collins and his team of researchers looked at pairs of companies in the same industries that at one time had been fairly similar, but at some point one company had gone from "good to great" while the other had been left behind. The goal was to find the principles or practices that made the difference.

One of those principles came to be known as the Stockdale Paradox. It was named for Admiral Jim Stockdale, who was a prisoner of war during the Vietnam War. Collins had interviewed Stockdale at one time and asked him how he was able to live through such a horrible experience, while others seemingly younger and more fit wound up dying in the prison. Stockdale noted that the prisoners who were either complete optimists or complete pessimists had the most trouble surviving. It was the ones like him that combined realism with a long view that finally made it out.

In his book, Collins notes that great companies approach their world in a way that is very similar to how Stockdale approached being a POW. Collins names the principle the Stockdale Paradox, and outlines it like this: "You must retain faith that you will prevail in the end, regardless of the difficulties. AND at the same time . . . You must confront the most brutal facts of your current reality, whatever they might be."[17]

Christian blogger Bruce Maples wonders, "If we substitute 'God will prevail in the end' in the first part, can we then use this as a starting point for an adult view of faith?" Ask yourself, "*If* I really believe that God and

God's ways win in the end, what does it mean for me today? Should it affect my thinking, or my actions? Should it change the decisions I make?"[18]

You see, "it would be easy to read Hebrews 11 and miss its central truth. Most of us read it and think of it as a list of great deeds by great people. (Which lets us off the hook for applying it to our own lives.) But what if the real point is that all these people shared one important attribute—they all believed that God is going to prevail in the end,"[19] that God's kin-dom will come to be on earth as it is in heaven, and in order for that to happen we have to live as kin-dom-builders; we have to live as if that kin-dom is already here on earth. For the people in the Hebrews's "Faith Hall of Fame," this conviction informed the decisions they made and the actions they took.

Maples applies the Stockdale Paradox to real-life situations to see how it affects the living of our faith:

> "My workplace is full of back-biting and fights to get ahead"—but God will prevail—and I am connected to God—so I will love even the back-biters and find my security in God, [not my job].'
>
> 'My family is falling apart'—but God will prevail—and I am called to bring the love of God into my family—so I will neither gloss over the issues, nor give up on the possibility of re-birth, but will be a constant source of love, openness, and honesty.[20]

This kind of faith:

> combines a central, core belief in the existence and ultimate triumph of God and God's ways, with a realistic appraisal of the world today. It then acts in accordance with God's ways, even when it seems counter-intuitive, in order to affect the current reality and move it toward God's reality [God's kin-dom].
>
> . . . [Faith] is not something we have to have 'enough of' in order to do things, or change things, or be this or that. It is not some sort of magic potion, or some mental fake-out. [Faith is] a quiet, firm conviction that in spite of whatever evidence our current reality tries to throw at us . . . there is a God, that God is loving and good, and that loving and good God is both the Ground of All Being and the Ultimate Winning Reality.[21]

Whoever you are and wherever you are on your journey of faith . . . *Can you celebrate the faith* of your forefathers and foremothers that brought you here?

Can you consider a faith that is grounded in reality but that lives and moves and has its being in a different reality: the reality—or fantasy—of God, our great Dreamer and Creator? *Can you commit to a faith*, whether it's as small as a mustard seed or so strong that it can move mountains (Matthew 17:20), that will always and forever anchor you to hope?

The good news is: celebrating, considering, and committing to such a faith is a hopeful and hope-filled enterprise because *it's not all up to us.*

Spiritual writer Henri Nouwen received a great revelation about faith at the circus, of all places! Nouwen went to see a performance by the German trapeze group The Flying Rodleighs. He was mesmerized by their breath-taking performance as they flew gracefully through the air. At the end of the show, he spoke with the leader of the troupe, Rodleigh himself. Nouwen asked him how he was able to perform with such grace and ease so high in the air. Rodleigh responded, "The public might think that I am the great star of the trapeze, but the real star is Joe, my catcher . . . The secret is that the flyer does nothing and the catcher does everything. When I fly to Joe, I have simply to stretch out my arms and hands and wait for him to catch me. The worst thing the flyer can do is try to catch the catcher. I'm not supposed to catch Joe. It's Joe's task to catch me."[22]

My brothers and sisters, God will catch you with whatever faith you have or don't have. In fact, if anything, the Hebrew's "Faith Hall of Fame" is as much or more a testimony to God's enduring faith in us, as it is of our enduring faith in God. That kind of faith—God's faith in us, not our faith in God—is the very heart of hope.

Amen.

Notes

1. Rabbi Shais Taub, "Faith vs. Fantasy" *HuffPost Religion Blog*, August 16, 2015, http://www.huffingtonpost.com/rabbi-shais-taub/faith-vs-fantasy_b_932656.html (accessed August 20, 2015).

2. Ibid.

3. David E. Gray, "Hebrews 11:1-3, 8-16: Pastoral Perspective", eds. David L. Bartlett and Barbara Brown Taylor, *Feasting on the Word: Preaching the Revised Common Lectionary*, Year C, Volume 3 (Louisville, KY: Westminster John Knox Press, 2010), 330.

4. Ibid.

5. John C. Shelley, "Hebrews 11:1-3, 8-16: Theological Perspective", eds. David L. Bartlett and Barbara Brown Taylor, *Feasting on the Word: Preaching the Revised Common Lectionary*, Year C, Volume 3 (Louisville, KY: Westminster John Knox Press, 2010), 328.

6. Laurence DeWolfe, "The Hall of Fame of Faithfulness," *Presbyterian Record: Progressive Lectionary*, July 1, 2013, http://presbyterianrecord.ca/2013/07/01/the-hall-of-fame-of-faithfulness/ (accessed August 16, 2015).

7. Thomas G. Long, "Hebrews," ed. James Luther Mays, *Interpretation: A Bible Commentary for Teaching and Preaching* (Louisville, KY: Westminster John Knox Press, 1997), 115.

8. Long, "Hebrews," 115–16.

9. The pseudepigrapha includes Enoch 1, Enoch 2, and Enoch 3.

10. Long, "Hebrews," 116–17.

11. Long, "Hebrews," 117–18.

12. Long, "Hebrews," 118–19.

13. Long, "Hebrews," 119–20.

14. Rev. Henry Williams, Jr., "Faith vs. Fantasy," *CenLa Focus*, October 2011, http://www.cenlafocus.com/faith/faith-vs-fantasy/ (accessed August 16, 2015).

15. Ibid.

16. Ibid.

17. Bruce Maples, "Can We Get a Grown-Up View of Faith?" *BruceWriter.com*, August 4, 2013, http://brucewriter.com/a-grown-up-view-of-faith-hebrews-11/ (accessed August 16, 2015).

18. Ibid.

19. Ibid.

20. Ibid.

21. Ibid.

22. Henri J.M. Nouwen, *The Only Necessary Thing: Living a Prayerful Life* (New York: The Crossroad Publishing Company, 1999), 195–96.

14

The Face at the Finish Line

Hebrews 12:1-17

Hebrews 12 compares our journey of faith to that of a race that we run with perseverance and endurance our whole lives long. We partner up with "surrounding witnesses," pressing on, not toward a finish line, but to a familiar face—that of Jesus Christ. A marathon serves as the metaphor for how we might think of running the Christian race in new ways, paying attention to the beat of our own hearts as well as paying attention to the runners around us. Rather than running toward the Jesus that lives in history or in heaven, what if we ran toward the living Christ who dwells within us? What if we found that finding God and finding our true self was actually the same thing? Discover how our faith journeys require an enduring hope that equips us to go deeper into the heart of who we really are. It is the journey into our hearts that will lead us to the heart of Christ. And ultimately this journey is about compassion, not competition.

Andrew: Many of us are turning our attention to our beloved Broncos and raising our hopes that our quarterback will be able to once again "run with perseverance the race that is set before him" (12:1). And how timely it is that since we are turning our attention toward the sports arena, so is the preacher of Hebrews in today's text.

Just last week, we heard the preacher of Hebrews recall the holy heroes in the spiritual hall of fame. Those faithful from one generation to the next form a ring of honor that links Noah and Abraham and Sarah to Moses and David and Samuel and the Prophets, and ultimately to Jesus, whom the book of Hebrews calls "the pioneer and perfecter of our faith" (12:2). It is a great chain of faith unbroken across time by those who have linked arms and joined hearts in the never-ending journey toward the heart of God, fully revealed in the face of Jesus; the one who anchors us in hope by the "once for all sacrifice of himself."

Now, the metaphor shifts a little, and Hebrews 12 compares our journey of faith to that of a race that we run with perseverance and endurance our whole lives long. We play our part in the great relay race of faith—we have been set up for spiritual success by "surrounding witnesses"—those who have taken their place in that great Sports Authority field in the sky and who are watching and waiting for us, cheering us on toward the finish line. Even more so, we learn the rules of the race by the one who teaches us how to run in the first place: Jesus, who has shown us how to run the course with patience and perseverance and endurance and flawless form. He is the one who sets the pace and shows us how to dash and sprint when we have to, how to handle the long hills of grief and challenge and change, how to slow down and take a rest when we are sucking wind in our daily lives, or when our faith becomes dehydrated and we suffer spiritual or emotional ACL injuries or cramps of doubt and fear and shame.

As we've learned through the experience of the congregation in Hebrews, the race is hard. Our muscles get sore for one reason or another. Our cardio capacity is not what we thought it was, so we can become tired and lose heart and lose confidence that we can finish the race we're running, no matter how many pairs of running shoes we own or how long we've subscribed to Runner's World and no matter how many Clif bars we might eat (spiritually speaking). To translate the metaphor: running the race that is living out our faith is difficult, no matter how many years we've gone to church or how many Bibles we own or how many times we've received Communion. Perhaps this difficulty is a reason Hebrews gives this pep talk, "Therefore lift your drooping hands and strengthen your weak knees, and make straight paths for your feet, so that what is lame may not be put out of joint, but rather be healed" (12:12-13).

I have to admit that this metaphor of running a race is a real stretch for me. I've never been much of a runner, though I've tried in fits and starts to become one. Even so, part of the point Hebrews wants to make with the congregation and with us is that no matter how much pain we may feel when it comes to the discipline of running or parenting or even faith itself, the payoff is what Hebrews calls the "peaceful fruit of righteousness to all who have been trained by it" (12:11). Isn't peace a quality worth having? All of us would probably say that we want more peace in our lives. Hebrews is intent on the congregation creating a culture and climate of peace by the way they treat one another and by the way they endure the suffering of hostility or public shame. The preacher exhorts the Hebrews to "endure trials for the sake of discipline. God is treating you as children; for what child is there whom a parent does not discipline?" (12:7).

Of course, we know enough by experience that being disciplined is one of those things we could all agree is worthwhile, but we don't always have the energy or focus or time to accept it. This is the case with the physical discipline of exercise or eating as well as the spiritual disciplines of things like prayer and meditation, forgiveness, gratitude, spiritual parenting, Sabbath rest, and hospitality, just to name a few.

Cultivating these acts of discipline is so difficult when we face hardships and resistance of different kinds. The people of Hebrews were facing similar struggles. We hear in today's text that they faced hostility "that had not yet resulted in bloodshed" (12:4), but they faced forces nonetheless that would keep them discouraged and tired and that would make them want to throw up their hands and quit. Instead, the preacher of Hebrews turns their attention to Jesus once again as the standard bearer of how to act when facing circumstances of this kind: he "endured the cross, disregarding its shame . . . " (12:3).

Maybe the people of Hebrews are saying, "I just want to run away from it all!" But as writer Samuel Shoemaker once wrote, "A strange man on the cross won't let me."

The wisdom of Hebrews, if I could summarize some, is that there is an acceptance of hardship that is not admitting defeat. In fact, it's part of running the race and being surrounded by the great cloud of witnesses that are well acquainted with suffering, both the world's and their own. The face at the finish line of our lives and our faith is the one we are pursuing all along, whether we know it or not.

Christ comes to us the same way. I was reminded of this truth this past week. *GQ* ran a profile on Stephen Colbert titled "The Late Great Stephen Colbert," checking in with the comedian (and, according to the article, "one of the country's few public moral intellectuals") before he kicks off his much-anticipated stint as host of *The Late Show* in September. The article starts out with a story about Colbert needling Eminem on a public-access show in Michigan. All of a sudden, Colbert is dropping assertions like, "people's suffering is sacred," perhaps because the interviewer was Joel Lovell of *This American Life* fame.

In this interview, Colbert says, "I was left alone a lot after Dad and the boys died . . . And it was just me and Mom for a long time . . . And by her example am I not bitter. By *her* example. She was not. Broken, yes. Bitter, no."[1]

"Maybe, he said, she had to be that for him. He has said this before—that even in those days of unremitting grief, she drew on her faith that the only way to not be swallowed by sorrow, to in fact recognize that our sorrow is inseparable from our joy, is to always understand our suffering, ourselves, in the light of eternity. What is this in the light of eternity? Imagine being a parent so filled with your own pain, and yet still being able to pass that on to your son."[2]

"It was a very healthy reciprocal acceptance of suffering," Colbert said. "Which does not mean being defeated by suffering. Acceptance is not defeat. Acceptance is just awareness." He smiled in anticipation of the callback: "'You gotta learn to love the bomb,'" he said. "Boy, did I have a bomb when I was 10. That was quite an explosion. And I learned to love it. So that's why. Maybe, I don't know. That might be why you don't see me as someone angry and working out my demons onstage. It's that I love the thing that I most wish had not happened. . . ."[3]

The interviewer asked Colbert if the comedian could help him understand that better, and he described a letter from Tolkien in response to a priest who had questioned whether Tolkien's mythos was sufficiently doctrinaire, since it treated death not as a punishment for the sin of the fall but as a gift. "Tolkien says, in a letter back: 'What punishments of God are not gifts?'" Colbert knocked his knuckles on the table. "'What punishments of God are not gifts?'" he said again. His eyes were filled with tears. "So it would be ungrateful not to take *everything* with gratitude. It doesn't mean you want it. I can hold both of those ideas in my head."[4]

Colbert said that he was 35 before he could really feel the truth of this sentiment.

What gives us strength and energy to run this race to completion and not just start it is this sort of wisdom about endurance through suffering, perseverance through hardships, and knowing that all along we are not alone in our race of faith

New Testament scholar Tom Long provides a useful analogy:

> In many major cities there are annual marathons involving thousands of runners. At the head of the pack are the world-class marathoners. Lean and speedy, they race through the course with astonishing swiftness.

At the rear of the throng, however, the picture is quite different. There we find the ordinary runners, a few more years under the belt perhaps, a little extra weight over the belt, a lot more pausing to sip water and to catch one's breath. There are also the contestants on crutches and in wheelchairs, courageously out on the course nonetheless. Sometimes one of the runners near the back will grow weak from the heat or faint from exhaustion. When this happens, other runners will stop to help out, compassion being more important than competition in the rear of the marathon.[5]

This is the face of what running the spiritual race is all about. We are called like the people of Hebrews to do likewise. Lord knows that we are all small links in the much bigger chain of faith. And the face at the finish line really becomes the faces of all of us—the faces of Jesus in disguise as Mother Teresa would say. We are to be Christ to one another, after all. That's what a community like ours is ultimately all about—in good times and bad; in sickness and in health; for richer and for poorer, and especially in those times when we feel that we are one of the ones at the back of the pack. If we don't give up, if we keep confidence and don't lose heart, we'll find the words of Jesus to be true all over again, "The first shall be last, and the last shall be first." And so may it be for us, between the start line and the finish line. If I have to, you have to stay in the race.

Amen.

Notes

1. Joel Lovell, "The Late Great Stephen Colbert," Gentleman's Quarterly, August 17, 2015, http://www.gq.com/story/stephen-colbert-gq-cover-story (accessed August 20, 2015).

2. Ibid.

3. Ibid.

4. Ibid.

5. Thomas G. Long, "Hebrews," ed. James Luther Mays, *Interpretation: A Bible Commentary for Teaching and Preaching* (Louisville, KY: Westminster John Knox Press, 1997), 134–135.

15

Shaking Things Up

Hebrews 12:18-29

In her book, *The Great Emergence*, Phyllis Tickle makes the case that Christianity has gone through a "rummage sale" of faith about every 500 years where old ideas are rejected and new ones emerge. The result is a refreshed and renewed Christianity that can grow with more vitality and strength—until it's time for another rummage sale, of course. 2,000 years after Jesus, we are in the midst of one of these "500-year rummage sales of our faith," and it is reason for hope! Hebrews 12 says something similar: God will give us "one last shaking, meaning a thorough housecleaning, getting rid of all the historical and religious junk so that the unshakable essentials stand clear and uncluttered," (v. 27, *The Message*). If this is true, what about Christianity as if exists right now would you keep? What would you shake up or throw out? What would it take for your own faith to be renewed and revitalized?

Anne: When I was in first grade, my family got a white fluffball of a puppy that I named "Cuddles." Cuddles was a great pet throughout my childhood and teen years; she died sometime when I was in college. Fast forward to this summer. Damon and I get our first dog, a golden retriever puppy that we named "Deacon." A month ago I got a package in the mail from my mom with this Frisbee in it. The note said something like, "This was one of Cuddles' first toys, and now it can be one of Deacon's first toys too. We hope he enjoys it as much as Cuddles did!"

This is either really cool or really creepy! My mom sent me my dead dog's toy Frisbee that was bought probably 26 years ago, and Cuddles has been dead at least 12 years, maybe more.

Who keeps stuff like this?

My mom. My mom keeps stuff like this. (And since I know my mom will watch this sermon later, "Thanks Mom. Deacon loves the Frisbee.")

Andrew: What about you? What kind of stuff do you hang on to? What is the weirdest thing you have saved for sentimental value? And for all you down-sizers in the room: what was the hardest thing for you to get rid of?

Anne: We all have criteria we use to determine what to save and what to sell, what to keep and what to give away:

- Do you keep stuff because of its **sentimental** value, the memories that give it meaning?
- Do you keep stuff because of its **functionality**, how practical it is?
- Do you keep stuff because of its **financial value**, because you paid a pretty penny for it or because you think it's worth a pretty penny should you one day decide to sell it?
- Do you keep stuff because **somebody else wants you to** (i.e.: the tea set that your wife never uses but always thinks she will some day)?
- Do you keep stuff not because you want to keep it really, but just because **you can't bear to get rid of it**?

How do you decide what criteria to use and when to use it? The same questions I just asked you about your stuff can also be asked about your theology:

Do you hang on to theology not because it makes sense but because it's in all the good ole hymns you sang growing up or because a pastor or parent told it to you?

Do you go to this church just because your spouse or partner is Baptist so now you're Baptist too?

Is your faith the heart of who you are and all you do, *or* is it something that you can throw to the wayside without really caring if you ever find a replacement for it?

Does your faith, as it stands today, function well for you? Is it forcing you to put God in a box, or is it freeing you to experience God's blessing?

Tending to our faith is a life-long process. If we downsize and/or upgrade our theology and belief system along the way in life, rather than waiting until we're forced to do so in a time of crisis, then there's far less chance a major spiritual earthquake will split the foundation of our faith.

However, a hearty shake up of things every now and again is a good thing. Just look at Hebrews.

Midway through chapter 12, the preacher of Hebrews begins the "final exhortation"[1] of his sermon. Using Mount Sinai and Mount Zion as metaphors of the spiritual journey, the preacher lights a fire under his people.

He uses Mount Sinai to sum up all he's said so far about the exodus, the wilderness wanderings, the levitical priestly system, the first covenant, and all the unfulfilled longings of the people of God. He recasts the details of the appearance of God at Sinai as told in Exodus 19–20 and Deuteronomy 4–5 in a new light. Shining the light of the new covenant on the dark shadows of Sinai reveals not a positive experience of God, but a distant and inaccessible one. The experience on Sinai includes natural disasters, trumpet blasts, and a frightening voice speaking without face or form.[2] On Sinai, the people beg Moses not to let God speak to them directly because, as they say, "We will die" (Ex 12:19). Even Moses himself shook with fear in the presence of God (Ex 12:21; Deut 9:19).[3]

The preacher of Hebrews contrasts this terrifying experience of God on Sinai to the jubilant experience he claims his listeners have: the experience of being pilgrims on a journey to Mount Zion, which is "the heavenly Jerusalem in festive assembly with God, [and] with Jesus, whose self-offering has made possible this [direct] accessibility to God's presence with all the saints and angels in joyful song."[4] Sounds delightful, right? This is why the posture on Mount Zion is not one of fear and trembling for being judged for your misdeeds, but one of great rejoicing and worship in awe and reverence of the One who has come as the final judge for us all and has only one verdict to give: "not guilty."[5]

In a way, the preacher is describing two diverging roads that go up two sides of the same mountain.[6] Both lead to God's presence, but the question is: what kind of experience do you want to have of God in your life? You can take the path of Mount Sinai and be afraid of God, cowering beneath God's thunderous voice, making sacrifices to constantly prove your worth, and dodging lightning strikes along the way. *Or* you can take the path of Mount Zion, a path where you travel with the company of fellow pilgrims and are "surrounded by so great a cloud of witnesses" (12:1). When you arrive, you meet God in the person and priest of Jesus Christ, who has forgiven our sins forever through his "once and for all" (Hebrews 7:27) sacrifice, freeing us to sing praises and worship God with fullness of heart, mind, body, and soul.

That doesn't mean the path of Mount Zion is all hunky-dory though. There's still all that stuff about a fiery shakedown at the end of chapter 12 we have to deal with. There was fire on Sinai, but there is fire on Zion too. Preacher Tom Long describes the difference, saying:

> Zion and Sinai are an eternity apart; one is the mountain of the new covenant and the other the old. It is true that, like Sinai, Zion has fire and shaking, but under the new covenant these experiences are transformed. Under the old order, fires and earthquakes are destroyers, burning up everything in their paths and shaking down all once-stable structures. Under the new covenant, though, God shakes the heaven and earth like an antique collector shakes the dust off an old marble statue: to get rid of everything that hides and defaces the beauty that was intended by the sculptor. In Zion, God shakes not to destroy but to preserve, 'so that what cannot be shaken may remain' (12:27). In Zion, God is a consuming fire: not a wildfire burning out of control, but a refiner's fire, purifying and preserving the righteous (Malachi 3:2-4), the fire that at the end of the age burns up 'all causes of sin and evil doers' (Matthew 13:40-43).[7]

The Message puts it plainly: "[God will] rock the heavens: 'One last shaking, from top to bottom, stem to stern.' The phrase 'one last shaking' means a thorough housecleaning, getting rid of all the historical and religious junk so that the unshakable essentials stand clear and uncluttered" (12:26-27).

Andrew: That our faith needs a good shaking every once and so often is not a new thought. It has been going on throughout the history of Christianity. Phyllis Tickle is an authority on religion in America and was the founding editor of the Religion Department of *Publishers Weekly*. In her 2008 book *The Great Emergence: How Christianity is Changing and Why*, she cites Anglican Bishop Mark Dyer's observation that "the only way to understand what is currently happening to us as twenty-first-century Christians in North America is first to understand that about every 500 years the church feels compelled to hold a giant rummage sale."[8]

Every 500 years there are shifts and changes in faith that require the church to go through its stuff. Some of us love going through our stuff—or other people's stuff—setting out on Saturdays for garage sales or staying home and cleaning out our attics. Others of us don't enjoy this in the least bit. Why? Well, because it's hard work. And there is emotion that we attach to stuff. And there is grief in letting go of our treasures—or our trash, for that matter.

But whether trash or treasure, that's part of the point of having a rummage sale or a garage sale or a yard sale. Sometimes this cleaning and clearing out process happens when we're moving. As you know, moving ranks right up there on the "major life changes anxiety meter," along with death and marriage! Even so, it is a kind of "necessary suffering," and as the church knows, it's not so much boxes and dishes and books and old photographs and toys and trinkets that we are rummaging through. It's a whole bunch of practices and beliefs or our ideas about the "right" way to worship or what the point of a spiritual community is really all about and ways of being church that are no longer effective and get in the way of being the life-giving presence of Christ that we are called to be in the first place.

And so the church holds these spiritual and theological rummage sales when it goes through what it has collected and the sends the extra baggage to recycling and keeps what is essential for the future. And again, it seems to happen every 500 years. You can think about it this way: 500 years ago was the Protestant Reformation. 500 years before that was the Great Schism (the division of the church into East and West); 500 years before that was the end of the Holy Roman Empire; and 500 years before that was the time of the revolution of Jesus. What Tickle and others believe is that we are now in one of those "every 500 years" moment, called the Great Emergence. It is a time of change. It is a time of shifting. It is a time of upheaval for the church as many of us have always known it. It is a time when Christian faith is getting a good shake.

Evidently a rummage sale was going on right here in Hebrews. Faith was getting a good shake even then. It is as if times of upheaval, whether it's the first century or the twenty-first, separate what is temporary from what is timeless. In the words of Hebrews: "At that time his voice shook the earth; but now he has promised, 'Yet once more I will shake not only the earth but also the heaven.' This phrase, 'Yet once more,' indicates the removal of what is shaken—that is, created things—so that what cannot be shaken may remain . . . we are receiving a kin-dom that cannot be shaken" (12:26-28a). And in these last verses of chapter 12, the psalmist joins in: "God is our refuge and strength, a very present help in trouble. Therefore we will not fear, though the earth should change, though the mountains shake in the heart of the sea" (Ps 46:2).

As it was with the people in the congregation of Hebrews, lightning and shaking mountains aside, this is a new era. Now is a fresh invitation to participate in the newness the unshakeable God is bringing about in the midst of shaky circumstances and a shaken world. We know that, even when the rest of the world (including the church) shutters and shakes, the ground of all of our confidence is in the unshakeable kin-dom of God.

Anne: What is true of the church "at large" is true for us as a local church too, albeit on a smaller scale. Maybe our shakedowns and rummage sales come every 5 years rather than every 500. If we picture Calvary as a microcosm of the jubilant community on Mount Zion, what do we see? What do we see as God's vision for us?

Do we need a good shake down? Are there ministries or programs that need to go through the refining fire of the Spirit to burn away what's already burnt out and give life to areas that are striving to thrive? Are there ways we can re-invigorate our church to become, even more, a community grounded in awe and reverent worship of God, especially as we are simultaneously open to all and closed to none? Are there ways we can re-invigorate ourselves to better encourage one another in small group faith formation, hands-on mission & service, and giving generously to all aspects of our ministry together because we so value what we receive from the people and programs of this place that we can't imagine our lives without it?

It's through getting our heads and hearts together that we begin to discover what we need to shake off as a church, and what we need to keep. If there's not congregational involvement in any given area, then that's a sign it's not a priority for us. The qualifier to this is that we don't necessarily always feel it is right to shake off the areas or programs where we are struggling to get volunteers. Sometimes the process is less of a shaking off of church programming and more a shaking off of our own individual lives and schedules to see if we are fulfilling our commitment to this community of which we chose to be a part!

For example, we all love and cherish one of the long-standing mission partners of our church, Family Promise, through which we house families experiencing homelessness for seven days at a time, 4-6 times a year. But the leaders would tell you it is getting to be more and more of a struggle to find sufficient volunteers to adequately staff the weeks we host families in our facility. The same people are volunteering, and they can't do it all. Thankfully people stepped forward at the last minute last week, but without the entire church pulling together to host these families, we have to evaluate if and how we can continue to be a host site as we have been. If it's like pulling teeth to get volunteers for something, what is that saying?

And you all know that it's been a struggle to find volunteers for our nursery and children's classes. But without adults physically present in the East Wing, we can't care for the kids who are physically present! Are we called to have a children's ministry at Calvary? Are we called to be a host site for Family Promise? I hope. But it's not up to me. Only we as a whole—collectively through each one of us asking ourselves if we can serve—will be able to answer this question.

When we reach our limit, we've reached our limit, but I don't know about you—I want to be 100% sure that each and every one of us has done a gut-check to make sure we're doing all we can do and that we've given all we can give and that we've prayed all the prayers we can pray and that we've invited all the people to church that we can invite before we start our rummage sale. After we've each done that, we can break out the yard sale signs and really evaluate what stays and what goes.

Because we can't do it all and no church should try to do it all, we must work together to discern what God is calling us to do. The question is not what do *we want* for ourselves, but what does God want for us? If we truly allowed the refining fire of the Holy Spirit to sweep over our congregation today, what would it burn and what would arise from the ashes with new purpose and presence? Like the fire on Mount Zion, this is an exciting process, not a dreadful one, even if there's still some fear and trembling along the way. Because ultimately, as we follow Christ's leading, it leads us more and more into the very presence of God.

Andrew: Lately I've been watching the old sitcom *Frasier*—about the witty and successful Dr. Frasier Crane who moves from Boston to Seattle to get a new start on life. In one episode, Frasier is tired of having his father Martin's old, shabby chair in his apartment filled with fine furniture, so he and his pretentious brother Niles go to a furniture store to purchase a new one—and they find one that even has a massage element to it. Thinking his dad would love it, Frasier actually gets himself into trouble when he throws out Martin's old chair.

What Frasier didn't realize was that Martin had an extreme sentimental attachment to the chair—the one that had to be held together with duct tape. Apparently, the chair was a memento to the many joys and sorrows in Martin's life, and Frasier had no idea of that deep meaning when he went to throw it out.

And after a bunch of bickering and fighting over the 25-year-old broken-down chair, it turns out that it's really not about a 25-year-old broken-down chair held together by duct tape. Frasier tells Martin that he will get him *any* chair he wants, and Martin says to Frasier, "Okay, I'll tell you what chair I want. I want the chair I was sitting in when I watched Neil Armstrong take his first step on the Moon. And when the US hockey team beat the Russians in the '80 Olympics. I want the chair I was sitting in the night you called me to tell me I had a grandson. I want the chair I was in all those nights, when your mother used to wake me up with a kiss after I'd fallen asleep in front of the television. Y'know I still fall asleep in it. And every once in a while, when I wake up, I still expect your mother to be there, ready to lead me off to bed. . . . Oh, but never mind. It's *only* a chair."[9]

You can see that, in the rummage sales of our personal lives, it is no casual matter what we decide to keep and what we decide to recycle or throw out altogether.

I wonder what your version is of Martin Crane's 25-year-old, rickety, broken-down chair. Sometimes the things that are of immense value to us go deeper than what meets the eye. Martin's old chair gives us a chance to ask about our own treasures (the spiritual kind, I mean): What is it that I need to never let go of? I grew up in a revivalist, evangelical culture that I no longer identify with anymore. It has taken me years to understand that just because my spiritual expression and understanding has become more contemplative and even "heady" in a way, I don't want to lose the "heart" of my first experiences of God. No matter the theology of it, I can hear an old gospel song and cry at the drop of a hat because there is something about the passion and heart of it that moves me deeply, even after all of these years.

What about you? What is it that you need to never let go of? What is it about your faith and your spiritual life that is timeless to you? What is so essential to your faith that without it you would be lost or shaken up?

And on the other side: What is it in your own life that you need to shake off? (And now that catchy Taylor Swift tune "Shake if Off" is running through many of our minds. Sorry about that!) But seriously. What is it time to release in your life? What is it time to let go of? Are there beliefs and practices that no longer work for you? Are there emotional attachments to some things that need to be released so that healing can happen for you?

When our faith is given a good shake, the purpose of the process is to be passionate followers of Jesus rather than passive supporters. Whatever reshaping or refashioning that has to happen for the renewal of the church to really happen begins with *us*. And it involves the shaking off of what is temporary so that what is timeless can remain—the timelessness of generosity and gentleness and faith and peace and every quality that cultivates in us a Christ-like attitude and spirit that leads us closer and closer to the heart of God and closer and closer to finding our true selves in God.

Whatever it is that is being shaken up in your personal life or even in your emotional and spiritual life these days, what was true then for the people of Hebrews is true now for we the people in this room—"since we are receiving a kin-dom that cannot be shaken, let us give thanks, by which we offer to God an acceptable worship with reverence and awe" (12:28).

As we do, let us embrace as fully and deeply as we can the timeless treasures that keeps us always near to the heart of God, and let us in the words of Hebrews "lay aside every weight and the sin that clings so closely, and let us run with perseverance the race that is set before us, looking to Jesus the pioneer and perfecter of our faith . . . " (12:1-2).

Amen.

Notes

1. Fred B. Craddock, "The Letter to the Hebrews: Introduction, Commentary, and Reflections," *The New Interpreter's Bible*, Volume XII (Nashville, TN: Abingdon Press, 1998), 156.

2. Ibid.

3. Thomas G. Long, *Hebrews: Interpretation: A Bible Commentary for Teaching and Preaching* (Louisville: John Knox Press, 1997), 137–38.

4. Craddock, 156

5. Long, 138.

6. Ibid, 136.

7. Ibid, 139–40.

8. Tom Roberts, "The Inevitable, Necessary Crisis," *National Catholic Reporter*, May 13, 2009, http://ncronline.org/news/faith-parish/inevitable-necessary-crisis (accessed August 29, 2015).

9. "John Mahoney: Martin Crane," quote from "Frasier," season 1, episode 19: "Give Him the Chair!" March 17, 1994, https://www.imdb.com/title/tt0582414/characters/nm0001498 (accessed February 11, 2020).

16

Here's the Heart of It

Hebrews 13

The author of Hebrews wraps up a challenging book of Scripture with a chapter that essentially outlines, in very plain and simple terms, what is essential in our faith. The author lets us know what matters most when it comes to the love of God, the message of Jesus, and the church of Christ. Here we have the heart of Hebrews as the benediction of hope through Jesus coming to fully share our human sufferings, committing to labors of love, transforming those he calls "brothers and sisters," and then being raised by God from the dead. Hebrews all along has been revealing what gives rise to the hope found in this final chapter, an utterly practical commitment to live the way of Jesus and to embody God's bold hope for the world.

Anne: This final chapter of Hebrews sounds a bit different than the previous chapters doesn't it? It's plainer, more straightforward. Chapter 13 is the "so what" of the sermon, the "life application" portion of the preaching, the "take home test" of this grand theological treatise. In chapter 13, the preacher stops being preachy and he gets personal with his people. This is a refreshing change, and it comes just in time, because the people surely were starting to feel a bit over-stuffed with theology.

It's like each chapter of Hebrews is its own meaty dish in this long, drawn out 12-course feast that the preacher has prepared to feed his faith-hungry people. Each chapter has a different flavor to it, each with different nutritional value in this nuanced Christology that the preacher is conveying to his listeners in hopes that they will be convinced and re-committed to Christ, and therefore the church.

The Hebrews have dined patiently (and so have we!) on this twelve-course, twelve-chapter meal that the preacher has laid out for us of his high-priest Christology, which is supposed to persuade us all to jump back on the Jesus bandwagon, forget our disillusions with the church, and keep on keeping on through persecution and suffering, fatigue and failure. We've listened attentively and digested slowly as the preacher has gone on and on about deep and complex stuff, each chapter filling us with something new and even more bazaar at times.

Here's a re-cap of the menu:

- The flittering and fluttering of angels around Jesus who "sits at the right hand of the Majesty on high" (1:3)
- The suffering and testing of Jesus who was, for a little while, "made lower than the angels" (2:9)
- The hardened hearts of the Hebrew ancestors (ch. 3)
- The effort it takes to accept the gift of Sabbath rest (ch. 4)
- The great high priest, Jesus, who "sympathizes with our weaknesses" (4:15) and gives us "mercy and grace in times of need" (4:16)
- The need for "milk," not "solid food," when we become "dull in our understanding" as students of the faith (5:11, 13-14)
- The "sure and steadfast anchor of our soul," (6:19) which is hope (ch. 6)
- The mystery around King Melchizedek that becomes a metaphor for Christ (ch. 7)
- The old covenant/new covenant comparisons and the new covenant/old covenant comparisons (ch. 8)
- The "once for all" (9:26) sacrifice of Jesus that trumps the never-ending sacrifices of animals (ch. 9)
- The fulfillment of Jeremiah's prophecy of "writing the laws on their hearts and minds" (10:16) through the person of Jesus whose life makes us "consider how to provoke one another to good deeds" (10:24)
- "The assurance of things hoped for," which is faith, and "the conviction of things not seen," which is faith as seen in the lives of the Hebrew heroes who lived "by faith": Abel, Enoch, Noah, Abraham, Sarah, Isaac, Jacob, Joseph, Moses, Rahab, Gideon, Barak, Samson, Jephthah, David, Samuel, the prophets, and the hosts of others (11:1)
- "The cloud of witnesses" that surrounds us, allowing us to "lay aside every weight and the sin that clings so closely" so we may "run with perseverance the race that is set before us" while looking to Jesus, "the pioneer and perfecter of our faith," as we leave behind the path of Mt. Sinai and choose instead the path of Mt. Zion, shaking away

that which is stale and self-serving so that we can worship God with awe and reverence and with fullness of body, mind, heart, and soul (12:1-2)

After the twelve meaty courses in this theological feast of faith, finally, we get to the after dinner mint—the refreshing change of taste, and pace, of chapter 13. The part that allows us to savor and soak up all that we have taken in, preparing us to head into our lives using the nourishment we have received to actually change something about the way we think, believe, live, learn, and love.

In chapter 13, the preacher of Hebrews finally tells us how to live like Jesus, who is the "reflection of God's glory and the exact imprint of God's very being" (1:3), so that our lives, too, become "imprints" of God's very being. If the heart of Hebrews is hope, and the heart of the Hebrew people is faith, then chapter 13 gives us reason to believe that our hearts, too, can be "holy partners in this heavenly calling" (3:1), living as "imprints" of God's love, grace, and hope in the world.

Because of the distinct change in the style and delivery of the text, some scholars have speculated about the possibility of different authorship for chapter 13. This is a hard claim to make when we don't know who the author of chapters 1–12 was to begin with, besides the fact that the heart of Hebrews, the theology and Christology, holds consistent and true from chapter 1 through chapter 13. We've said from week one that Hebrews is more like a sermon than a letter and its author is more like a preacher than a writer, and truly if it weren't for chapter 13, Hebrews probably wouldn't be called an "epistle" (or letter) at all. In chapter 13 we finally see the traditional elements of a letter that justify it as such: moral imperatives and instructions, a benediction, and a farewell. While chapter 13 resembles elements of the letters of the Apostle Paul, it is widely believed that Paul did not write Hebrews.[1]

However, the fact that Timothy is mentioned in the farewell sentences at the end and is referenced as being "set free" (13:23)—which means he probably had been in prison—gives reason to believe this Timothy is the same Timothy mentioned in Paul's other letters (Acts 16:1-3; 2 Cor 1:1, 19). All this means is that the author of Hebrews, while still a mystery, was probably at least on the "outer edges of the Pauline circle" of disciples and followers.[2]

Also in the farewell, we have mention of Italy, which is an exciting clue. Could we finally know where the preacher is? Well, not really. The phrase, "those from Italy send you greetings" (13:24) doesn't really tell us much because the preacher could be in Italy and saying, "all the Christians around me here say hello" *or* he could be somewhere else writing home to Italy saying "all the homesick Italians here with me say hello and wish they were there with you" *or* he could be in some other spot simply saying, "I'm with some immigrated Italians who live here and they want me to say hello."

Tom Long says,

> The geographical location of Hebrews may be obscure, but its theological location is not. We do not know where the Preacher is on the globe, but we do know where he stands on the map of faith. The last line of Hebrews tells everything: 'Grace be with all of you.' . . . this is the ultimate message of Hebrews, the ultimate message of the gospel. Because of the ministry of the great high priest, the great shepherd of [all] the sheep, grace is with all of you [no matter who you are or where you are on life's journey].[3]

Tom Long says it's as if the main sermon ended at chapter 12, and now in chapter 13, the preacher turns toward "the more routine aspects of congregational life: to the ministry of hospitality, the prison visitation program, the stewardship emphasis, and the like. In short, the sermon is being followed by the announcements and the 'joys and concerns.'"[4]

In other words, the living out of our faith, no matter our theology, consists of basic and essential elements, actions that reflect the love and life of Jesus—things that are part of our everyday life together. For example, with Calvary's tagline, "Being Open to All. Closed to None,"[5] we welcome guests into our congregation. The author of Hebrews says we are to "let mutual love continue" (13:1) by showing welcome and hospitality even "to strangers, for by doing that some have entertained angels without knowing it" (13:1-2). Maybe this means handing out bread to first-time guests or hosting homeless families in our church or handing out bags of food and grocery coupons to those who are hungry.

Through Peace & Justice Ministries, we carry out the exhortation that we are to care for those who are imprisoned or tortured (13:3), perhaps through writing letters about our Christian convictions on such things to our elected government officials or by writing letters of compassion and encouragement to those who are themselves in prison.

At Calvary, we are dedicated to faith formation. Similarly, Hebrews instructs that we are to keep our relationships, especially our marriages

(13:4), at the forefront of our priorities, perhaps by growing in faith together with our partner in small group Bible study and prayer groups.

In terms of stewardship, we are to "keep our lives free from the love of money and be content with what we have" (13:5). Interestingly, the two references the preacher uses here to talk about money are from the Old Testament (surprise, surprise). The first is, "I will never leave you or forsake you" (Deut 31:6) and the second is, "The Lord is my helper; I will not be afraid . . ." (Ps 118:6). Through these references it's as if he's suggesting that "the love of money is not so much the product of greed as it is the fear of abandonment," which means, Tom Long says, "that when Jesus grasps our one hand in love it frees us to open up the clenched other hand and let the money go."[6]

Furthermore, chapter 13:7-17 discusses the importance of worshiping and maintaining a healthy congregational life together. We don't know exactly the circumstances, but we can be certain something was happening in the congregation of the Hebrews. It seems that some members of the church were getting off track and needed the corrective guidance of "the leaders," and they are reminded to look to the lives of their leaders for inspiration on how to live. The preacher also does a quick review about two main issues that seem to be tripping them up:

1. Some folks were confusing grace with rules regarding food (13:9). He reminds them that people are nourished by grace, not regulations. The whole attempt to turn Christianity into a rule-based ritualistic religion is a failure of nerve, a shrinking back to the ways of the old covenant, not the freeing grace of the meal at the Lord's Table. (10:29)

2. The congregation has a problem with the public side—the "outside the camp" dimension—of the Christian faith. Some are not even coming to worship (10:25), and those who are don't want to show their faces out in the world. Why? Because when they leave the sanctuary they are liable to be "publicly exposed to abuse and persecution" (10:32-39). Small wonder then that they would like to redefine the Christian faith as a list of food rules (applicable behind closed doors) rather than as a comprehensive way of life that they have to live out in the open.

   Fred Craddock suggests that to go to Jesus "outside the camp" is to join Abraham and all the company of faith pilgrims who left a homeland in search of the homeland, who left a city in search of the city (11:8-16). By declaring themselves strangers and aliens on the earth, (11:13) they took on the abuse that goes with the life of a pilgrim, which is to be without identity, without status, without place in the world."[7] Are we willing to do the same? Or do we prefer to stay within our own walls? Are we really a pilgrim people or a programmed people—in love with where we are, who we are with, and what we are doing—without regard to where God is leading us, who else God is inviting us to be with, and what else God is calling us to do?

The preacher goes on to emphasize the importance of prayer, which is a point he illustrates when he asks the congregation for prayer for himself: "Pray for me . . . for us . . . we've done the best we can, and we have a clear conscience" (13:18). If the leader of the community is not afraid to say he needs prayer, then why should anyone else be?

Finally, the preacher concludes with the final blessing, or benediction, which includes key theological points of the whole sermon. The author of Hebrews restates that God is a "God of Peace" (13:20) "who led up Jesus from the dead" (13:20). In an important aside, we should note that the verb here is not really "brought back" from the dead but "led up" from the dead, encouraging us that we, too, can be led up by God in whatever circumstances we are in, as the Psalmist writes in 40:2: "He lifted me out of the slimy pit, out of the mud and mire; he set my feet on a rock and gave me a firm place to stand."

God will "Make you complete in everything good, so that you may do his will . . . working among us that which is pleasing in his sight" (13:21). God is at work in human lives doing things that please God.[8] That's a lovely thought, isn't it? God is working in us; it's not up to us on our own.[9]

The preacher uses this final chapter to sum up the heart of his message: love others like Jesus loved others and don't be afraid or embarrassed or fearful about living as a bold community of faith that works together on what it means to love others like Jesus did. There are commitments to being in such a community and there are leaders put in place to help encourage you in those commitments. And undergirding it all, both your faith and your faith community, is prayer . . . lots of prayer . . . and the grace and peace of God.

Andrew: And now we come to the benediction in Hebrews. (And the benediction of a worship service is my favorite part! For reasons other than what you might think).

The "bene-diction" is the "good word" that the preacher of Hebrews has been leading to all along the way. And his benediction is a benediction of hope; the benediction of hope through Jesus coming to fully share our human sufferings, committing to labors of love, transforming those he calls "brothers and sisters," and then being raised by God from the dead.

Indeed, hope is the heartbeat song of Hebrews. What is at the heart of Hebrews to me? That's the question. Let me try to answer it from my own heart as best I can.

First of all, Hebrews is an utterly practical message of hope for all of those who are tired and uninspired and feel like faith has become too cold or too bold or too fake or too dangerous or not worth it. And this chapter gets at the heart of it all for me: "Let mutual love continue. Show hospitality to strangers. Remember those in prison. Honor marriage. Keep free from the love of money. Be content. Don't be afraid. Respect leadership. Trust Jesus. Do good. Share what you have" (13:1-7; 15-16).

These are not casual, carefree matters. There is a sense of urgency to this. Because there is no time to "wait and see what happens." This is no time to shrink back. There is no time to wait and see if we should love each other. There is no time to wait and see if we should be generous. This is not a time to sit on our hands and "wait and see," Hebrews says all along. The future is now. And as a friend of mine once said to me, "Andrew, when our memories become greater than our dreams, the end is near."

Well, the preacher of Hebrews is doing everything that he can to persuade the people that their dreams need to be bigger and better and bolder than ever before.

Hebrews offers both a mix of tough love at times—hitting on touchy subjects like money and sex and extending hospitality to people who look homeless and hungry and hurt. He is stern and even severe at times. I think this is why the preacher of Hebrews can speak in such an open and candid manner with his congregation. Beyond the insults at the beginning of today's text—calling them babies and dull in understanding—and the threats and fear-inducing language in the middle of chapter 6—saying it is impossible to restore to repentance those who were once enlightened and then have fallen away—we finally get to the clincher: "Even though we speak in this way, beloved, we are confident of better things in your case, things that belong to salvation" (6:9).

Hebrews is profound in that the preacher reminds the people who they are. The preacher of Hebrews has been reminding them all along of who they once were: people who took care of the sick and took in the stranger. The preacher is reminding the people of their past, "coaching them up" so to speak about how confident and compassionate and steadfast amidst suffering that they had been. He encourages them to "recall those earlier days when, after you had been enlightened, you endured a hard struggle with sufferings, sometimes being publicly exposed to abuse and persecution, and sometimes being partners with those so treated. For you had compassion for those who were in prison, and you cheerfully accepted the plundering of your possessions, knowing that you yourselves possessed something better and more lasting" (10:32-34).

The preacher's message to the congregation in Hebrews is a lot like the message that we need to hear today for the present and the future of Calvary. There are times when we need some tough love, when we need a good "talking to." There are times when we need to be reminded of who we are, but we can't let the memories of our past be bigger or bolder or better than the dreams and hopes for our future. It is in *your* hands, dearly beloved. You have the same power to offer the sacrifice of praise and doing good and sharing what you have in the same spirit of Jesus Christ as the people in Hebrews did.

Now, my friends, is time for our own spiritual gut check. This is what Hebrews has been to me: a spiritual gut check that is helping me find a way of being more honest with God and with myself. A gut check on asking myself what really matters and facing the truth of what I find in that: the inspiration to be bold and to make bold decision, being empowered as a leader to lead by action and not just with words, and to not be afraid, but to trust my unknown future to the known Christ who raises hope in me even now like I've not quite felt before. It is my hope that you will feel that hope, too, Calvary. And take action. "Let mutual love continue. Show hospitality to strangers. Remember those in prison. Honor marriage. Keep free from the love of money. Be content. Don't be afraid. Respect leadership. Trust Jesus. Do good. Share what you have" (13:1-7, 15-16).

This is the heart of Hebrews to me. What is it to you? Where is *your* heart in all of this today?

Anne: The thing that has struck me most about Hebrews is its strong *convictions* in its certainty about things like hope and faith.

I tend to be a person that lives in the grey and likes the grey. When things get too black and white they start to feel too boxed in to me, too prescribed or predictable. With too much stuff set in stone, I fear that there's not enough stuff left up to the Spirit, and you all know how I am about the Spirit. I truly believe it's alive and at work within each one of us as individuals and among all of us together as a community of faith.

However, as a pastor, as a leader, there is a cost in leaving so much up to the Spirit. And the *cost* is that sometimes the convictions I believe whole-heartedly and desperately want you, my congregation, to believe whole-heartedly too, are left uncommunicated. Or, if they are communicated, I'm not as clear as I could be for fear of people thinking that they can't be part of this community if they can't live up to these convictions, which is the last thing I would ever want. You don't have to share my convictions to be part of Calvary, but you do need to know I have them and that I'm serious about them.

Some of you know that the senior pastor before Mary Hulst, Larry Loughhead, used to end his sermons by saying, "Think about that." The implication is, of course, that even though Larry had just shared a bunch of his thoughts with the church, they had a responsibility to go off and think about all that he said on their own, and to decide for themselves what they thought.

Even though I don't end my sermons with "Think about that," I understand the sermonic moment in the same way. I share some thoughts, or Andrew and I share some thoughts that have been formed by other scholars and commentators and current events and sports/TV/movie/music/literary references that have been culled through by prayer with the hope that you go off and think your own thoughts on the matter, not believe what I say at face value.

But I think by not always sharing my convictions forthrightly and with a kind of forcefulness of heart, I have let you down and let us down. Not because we are doing anything wrong, but because I haven't always challenged us to do things in a way that rightly reflects the love of Christ and rightly reflects the cost of being a community together.

It is easy to come to church and consume. To consume worship like you do a movie. To consume a small group like you do a class at school. To consume the bread and the cup like you do a meal around your own dinner table. To consume pastoral care like you do a good conversation with a friend.

The thing is, when we consume, whether we're consuming a TV show or a great meal, we are in a posture of receiving whatever it is we want to receive at that moment. If you don't like the TV show, you'll turn it off. If you don't like the food, you'll stop eating it. We all know what happens when we don't stop doing those things: we end up wasting a perfectly good evening watching bad TV, or we end up stuffed and bloated from food that wasn't worth the calories.

Well, consumption is not the posture we are to have before Christ. Conviction is. We must face Christ with a conviction that what we are doing right now in this very moment matters. Being in worship right now, today, matters, and not just for the numbers on our attendance rolls; it matters for the formation of your faith, and your children's faith. Worship matters for my faith too, and for the faith of all those around you. We can't worship on our own.

A posture of conviction means you worship not because you like the music or don't like the music, but because you feel deeply that God is receiving your song, your heart, and your prayers through worshipping together. Worship never has been about what any one of us likes or doesn't like. Worship is about spending pure, uninterrupted time focusing on being in the complete presence of God, which is not easy!

A posture of conviction means you commit to being a part of a small group or church Sunday school class (or to leading one!), because without such group study and accountability you know your faith will not grow as it could; it might even become stale or stagnate. Without small group connections, how else will your church community know the ups and downs of your life, praying for you along the way? Our prayer list is distributed for the whole church to read, but our prayer life is made up real live prayer happening in small groups throughout the week. I know the power of this prayer, as I have the privilege of listening to the Tuesday morning prayer breakfast pray for me and for our entire staff every single week. It's one thing to have people tell you they are praying for you. It's another thing to experience and hear that prayer firsthand.

A posture of conviction means you find a way to serve Christ in the church as a volunteer and outside the church with one of our mission partners. Why? Because the number one thing we are to do is "love others as Jesus loves us." Jesus, much to my dismay, didn't love others through writing notes of encouragement or good thoughts. Jesus loved others by pushing through crowds, breaking rules on the Sabbath, listening and attending to the needy person who interrupted his day, and by getting his hands dirty touching lepers, mixing mud and spit, pulling up fishing nets, breaking bread in strangers' homes, and washing the weathered feet of his disciples.

Why do we need to serve both inside and outside the church? Because Jesus came to point us toward God's kin-dom and help us bring God's kin-dom to earth as it is in heaven, and God's kin-dom is both inside and outside the church. We can't neglect our own ministry—which desperately needs your helping hands and time—and we can't neglect the ministry of our community, which is how we share Christ's love with the world.

A posture of conviction means you welcome all people because God loves all people. Period. We do this pretty well, Calvary. But we can always do better simply by listening to one another better, hearing our stories, caring about what matters to each one of us, and seeking to help meet those needs—member to member—rather than just referring them to a pastor. You are the pastors of Calvary. We, the pastoral staff, are pastors of the pastors.

A posture of conviction means you give money to the church, and not just a little but a lot. (Doesn't this church mean a lot to you? Then why would you not give "a lot" to it?) You know in your gut what "a lot" is to you: the tithe (10% of your income) is proportional. It's a great equalizing standard for us all because it doesn't matter how much money we make; we're all giving equally. But for some of us "a lot" isn't a tithe—it's more than that. And for some of you "a lot" is less than a tithe because you are barely scraping by. That's fine too. The point is that you give to the church in the same way you pay money to buy the groceries that you eat. The food that nourishes our bodies isn't free, and neither is the spiritual food that nourishes our souls.

The important question is: How important is your faith community? What is it worth to you?

We certainly heard from a lot of you when we were exploring the possibility of selling our building because people couldn't bear the thought of Calvary being anywhere else. Well, the only reason we were exploring that possibility was because of the financial situation we were in this past spring and are still in today. Can you bear the thought of Calvary not being around at all? Our building is old and things will keep breaking. Our staff is young and we will burn out and break down, unless we leave before that happens. Calvary could run on volunteers, it's just that that does not seem feasible because we struggle to get volunteers for a whole number of our ministries. Things were different 20 years ago; people volunteered at church. Now we're all spread too thin in so many other areas, it seems as if there's no time for long-term commitments in volunteering for the church unless you are retired (and we are grateful for you retired folks!).

But without volunteers, we rely more on staff. But we can't rely on staff unless we can pay that staff enough to keep them. And while a church can rely on staff leadership, it can't thrive without lay leadership across all areas of ministry.

A posture of conviction means you pray even when you don't know if it makes a difference or if anyone is listening. You pray because prayer is a signal that it's not all up to us, that God is leading us, not our own egos or wish lists. Prayer is humbling and centering. I don't know about you, but in the chaos of the world around us, I need centering prayer now in my life more than ever. Prayer helps us pare down our lives and pay attention to what's most important. Illness does the same thing: its stops our world and we re-prioritize. But we don't have to be ill to refocus. Prayer can help us do that too.

I guess the heart of what I'm saying is that I have convictions about what it means to be a part of this community of faith we call Calvary. And my convictions are all about the commitments we make to one another when we say we "go to Calvary." Do we just "go to church" here? Or is this truly "our church?" These commitments of worship, faith formation, service, welcome, generosity, and prayer are not arbitrary. They are practices that that draw us nearer to the heart of Christ, and in turn, nearer to the hearts of one another. Isn't that what life is about? Living from our heart and listening to the hearts of others because we are all loved so deeply by the heart of God? No exceptions.

I experience the heart of God here at Calvary. I wouldn't be here if I didn't. When things have been hard and I've wondered if I could keep going as your pastoral leader, I have drawn strength, again and again, from my deep belief that the mission of our church is reflecting the life and love and desires of Christ. I love you, Calvary. And I love God, and as I listen to God and seek discernment as your senior pastor, I know we need a re-commitment to these basic core convictions, or values, of our church and of the Christian life in general. In the midst of all the grey of life, they are the "black and white" practices that keep us anchored to hope, rooted in love, and reminded, again and again, of God's grace.

So there you have it. My convictions about what it means to be a follower of Christ in this church we call Calvary. Let's get up out of our consuming posture, and settle into a posture of conviction about our love for God and for this church. Think not of what you want from Calvary,

but what the ministry of Christ needs from you for Calvary. That's what I'm thinking about. And I need you to "think about that" too. Because this is what it means to "raise hope" in our church, community, and world: to not only live with faith, but to forever redefine how that faith is embodied in each generation, including our own. It's the heart of Hebrews and it's the heart of who we too. So let's not give up hope. There's too much at stake.
Amen.

Notes

1. Fred B. Craddock, "The Letter to the Hebrews: Introduction, Commentary, and Reflections," *The New Interpreter's Bible*, XII, (Nashville, TN: Abingdon Press, 1998), 161.

2. Thomas G. Long, *Hebrews: Interpretation: A Bible Commentary for Teaching and Preaching* (Louisville: John Knox Press, 1997), 148–49.

3. Long, 149.

4. Long, 142.

5. This is the tagline for our church, Calvary Baptist Church of Denver, and the examples that follow are ministries in our church.

6. Long, 144.

7. Craddock, 167.

8. Long, 147.

9. Ibid.

www.ingramcontent.com/pod-product-compliance
Lightning Source LLC
Chambersburg PA
CBHW071714090426
42738CB00009B/1767